RATED R

A Biblical Perspective On Dating, Relationships, Marriage, And Sexual Purity

STAN BELYSHEV

RATED R

A Biblical Perspective On Dating, Relationships, Marriage, And Sexual Purity

NextGen Leaders Academy

StanBelyshev.com

Paperback ISBN: 9798410031431
Kindle ASIN: B09RJFFNVS
Hardcover ISBN: 9798410036900
Library of Congress Control Number 2021923314

Book Cover Design: Jennifer Chernenko

CONTENTS

INTRODUCTION

When it comes to movies or television shows, we all have our favorite genres or actors and actresses to watch. And one of the basic concepts of any film or television show is its rating, so the viewer knows what to expect. According to FilmRatings.com, they outline the general standards for each film or show before they are released, which are as follows:

G – *General Audiences*

PG – *Parental Guidance Suggested*

PG-13 – *Parents Strongly Cautioned*

R – *Restricted*

NC-17 – *Adults Only*

Even though the ratings have changed dramatically over the years, they are still just basic guidelines for the viewer, and I wanted to apply the same principle to the title of this book. What exactly is *Rated R*? Is the content of this book appropriate for adult readers? No! Is there a lot of strong language and erotic illustrations in the book? No! Can my adolescent son or daughter read this? ABSOLUTELY YES!

We have reached the pinnacle of our history and humanity, with so much knowledge, information, and options that as carnal human beings with insatiable appetites, we don't know what to do with this massive influx of just about everything.

Our culture is changing at such a breakneck pace that you have to pinch yourself to make sure you're not dreaming. Some of these cultural shifts are beneficial, while others are lethal and destructive.

The fact that you have chosen to read this book indicates that you have a strong desire to gain a biblical perspective on dating, relationships, marriage, and sexual purity. And as you align your heart, mind, and spirit man with God's perfect will for your life, marriage, and family, you will be able to enjoy the fullness of His divine blessings, pleasure, and purpose in relation to the marriage covenant, as well as all of the pure sexual benefits that come with it.

This book's goal is to challenge, equip, mentor, and provide biblical clarity and perspective on the important topics of dating, relationships, marriage, and sexual purity. And the majority of this book was written during my twenty-one days of prayer and fasting, during which I believe the practical insight or truth you will gain from these pages will serve as a GPS for your life and walk with the Lord. Additionally, it will provide you with clarity, hope, confidence, and a sigh of relief. So, my friend, take a seat, grab a big bucket of popcorn, and enjoy this *Rated R* book.

1

THE RATED R MANUAL

As I stated in my introduction, the "R" stands for *real*, not *restricted*, and I would like to introduce you to the true Rated R Manual, which is the Bible. Without a doubt, the Word of God is the most trustworthy and real manual for all of humanity, full of truth, wisdom, direction, and the meaning of life. This same manual is jam packed of divine instructions that will significantly improve the quality of your life.

So, what is the most fundamental purpose of any manual? A manual is typically a booklet containing valuable information about a specific product that you have purchased, and the sole purpose of any manual is to provide some insight or educate the individual about this specific product. Furthermore, any manual will contain warning content or strict instructions on what you can and cannot do with this specific product. And if the user chooses to ignore, disobey, or disregard these critical instructions, there will be consequences. And sometimes, as a result of these consequences, the product is damaged or permanently broken.

This is also true for the Rated R Manual, which is God's perfect law, and those who choose to live in accordance with it will receive many blessings, joy, and fulfillment in life. Those who choose to ignore or disobey what the living Word has to say will have a life filled with problems, heartaches, stress, sleepless nights, and bondage. And in this chapter, I will challenge you to grasp the crucial truth that the Bible is the only *Real* book that is genuinely interested in serving as a guide and a blessing to anyone who wishes to use this manual as their daily GPS.

THE BIBLE IS THE MOST RATED R BOOK

As I previously stated, the meaning of the letter "R" gives us as God's children great hope because the living Word that we have in our lives is the *Real* truth, the ultimate *Real* authority, and the only *Real* hope for all of humanity. The words inscribed throughout the pages of the Bible are saturated with our heavenly Father's love. Packed with hope, promises, and an endless supply of blessings. Furthermore, the Bible promises eternal life to anyone who accepts Jesus as their personal Lord and Savior.

Because the Bible is the most *Rated R* book that can change and transform lives, it has also become a stumbling block for millions of people throughout history and has offended and continues to offend an infinite number of people. So, why such a stark contrast? For some, the truth is a breath of life, while for others, it is toxic smoke. Even Apostle Paul provided some insight into this by saying, "But we preach Christy crucified, to the Jews a stumbling block and to the Greeks foolishness."[1]

As a born-again child of God who genuinely loves the Lord, you must declare unequivocally that the Bible is your daily manual and that what is written in those precious pages is the *Real* truth. This truth discusses marriage, our sexuality, healthy and unhealthy relationships, and how to live a sexually pure life by walking in the fear of the Lord in great detail. And the Bible is replete with numerous examples of people who struggled with their sexuality and those who triumphed. And this is why the Bible will always be the most popular Rated R book out there. So, seize this *Real* truth, which will set your life on the path of righteousness and holiness unto the Lord.

"IT IS ONLY IGNORANCE THAT LEADS ANY CHRISTIAN TO BELIEVE THAT THE BIBLE DOES NOT ADDRESS EVERY ASPECT OF LIFE."

THE BIBLE IS NOT AN OUTDATED BOOK

I've heard far too many arguments and seen far too many social media posts claiming that the Bible is out of date or irrelevant to today's culture. It would be easy to believe that these arguments are primarily coming from nonbelievers, but to our surprise, many of them are coming from Christians. One of the reasons for such a delusory belief is that many so-called Christians do not read the Bible, which is full of life stories, kingdom principles, and commandments pertaining to relationships, friendships, marriage, and our sexuality.

The Bible is not an out-of-date book, but rather the most up-to-date book with the best advice, suggestions, and recommendations regarding dating, relationships, marriage, and our sexuality. Here are just a few Bible references that address these critical issues:

- *Our God the Creator has said, "It is not good that man should be alone."[2]*
- *Mary, Jesus' mother, was a virgin.*
- *King Solomon had seven hundred wives and three concubines (girlfriends).*
- *King David was enamored with Bathsheba and eventually committed adultery with her.*
- *Joseph was forced to have sexual relations with Potiphar's wife, from whom he fled.*
- *Jesus forgave the adulterous woman who was caught in the act.*
- *In the Garden of Eden, Adam and Eve were naked, and they had no shame.*
- *In the Bible, the word sexual appears 24 times, fornication 14 times, adultery 36 times, marriage 36 times, holiness 35 times, and family 138 times.*

Again, the above outline is only a portion of what the Bible says about our sexuality, sexual immorality, sexual purity, marriage, and healthy relationships. And if you can tune out the perverse voices that are coming through social media platforms, Hollywood, or relevant culture, you will be able to preserve your sexual purity before marriage, step into a Godly relationship, and have a blessed marriage that will last until your dying breath.

Allow this *Rated R* manual to become your friend, your counselor, your consultant, and your GPS for life, particularly as it relates to dating, relationships, marriage, and sexual purity. And by doing so, you will unlock all of heaven's blessings for your life as a single person or as a married person with children. God's *Real* Word will not let you down!

"THE LIVING WORD OF GOD IS AS ALIVE OR AS REAL IN YOUR LIFE JOURNEY AS YOU ALLOW IT TO BE."

RATED "R" RECOMMENDATIONS

- The Bible will always keep it real.
- Many have attempted to discredit or erase the Bible from history, but if you stick to this R-rated source, you will also be able to withstand any attack or opposition.
- God's living Word is as real as it gets.
- When all else fails, turn to the Bible, which will never let you down.
- The world will present you with its theories, opinions, suggestions, and relevant ideologies, but the Bible will present you with the truth.

2
THE FORBIDDEN "S" WORD

Every parent has stopped, corrected, and even disciplined their child whenever they use inappropriate or profane language. This is normal parenting, and every local church has its own form of parenting in which the senior pastor, elders, or church leaders oversee the culture, atmosphere, and what is taught in the local church. And, sadly, there are plenty of pastors, seasoned church members, and leaders who act as police officers, fining you if you discuss or preach about sensitive subjects or mention uncomfortable language.

Growing up in church as a teenager, I honestly never heard the word "sex" spoken behind the pulpit. I don't remember my parents ever using this word in our household. Furthermore, I rarely heard pastors or preachers discuss healthy relationships and the benefits of marriage. But most often, these are the phrases I remember the most: "Sex is sin!" "You should marry so you don't lust after the opposite sex." "Dating is not permitted because it pertains to this world." This was only a small sampling of the statements made from the pulpit. I've heard similar stories from a vast number of people in my generation.

You'd think this was a thing of the past, but to my surprise, there are still churches that are afraid to talk about or preach about sex or sexuality. And one of the issues here is that there are churches, pastors, and even parents who choose to ignore this vital subject, allowing the world, social media, friends, and academia to take the lead in teaching and educating our children and the younger generation about what sex and sexuality are. And in this chapter, I will shed some light on the fact that we, as God's creation, are sexual beings, as well as the fact that Adam and Eve were both naked when they were created. Buckle up, my friend, as we embark on this heart-pounding adventurous chapter!

YOU ARE A SEXUAL BEING

We have been taught that we are made up of three parts: body, soul, and spirit. And much emphasis has been placed in sermons, teachings, and conferences on how important each of those three areas is. But I have yet to come across a teaching or a sermon that outlines the fact that we are human beings, spiritual beings, and sexual beings. And to ignore or dismiss this truth is to do the Word of God a great disservice.

When our heavenly Father created Adam and Eve, the Bible states, "And they were both naked, the man and his wife, and were not ashamed."[1] The key words are, *naked* and *not ashamed*. So, nakedness is not a shameful thing, unless it occurs outside of a marriage covenant, in which case you will feel shame and guilt because the person with whom you just had sexual intercourse is not your spouse.

So, why is it that this one crucial verse is quickly dismissed? Because admitting that Adam and Eve were both naked and had no shame would make most pastors and preachers uncomfortable behind the pulpit, because common sense dictates that when two people of opposite sexes are naked, they will both become sexually aroused, which will naturally lead to a sexually romantic act.

Why do I want to take a moment here to emphasize how important it is that we, as God's divine creation, are also sexual beings? Because I was taught as a child that sex is only for married couples to have children, but no one ever taught me that sex is a gift from our heavenly Father that the husband and wife can enjoy to the fullest in a marriage covenant. Or I was never taught that these sexual desires or feelings I have for the opposite sex are normal, that God created people as sexual beings, and that all I need to do is control and manage this feeling by keeping my focus on my Creator and not allowing myself to be exposed to areas where I'm not supposed to be exposed.

Knowing that we are sexual beings should not be a surprise, but it may be for some. And my heart's desire is to shed some light on this biblical truth so that we do not feel condemned or judged that we are strange, or strange, simply because we have some attraction to the opposite sex. In a nutshell, every normal human being has the desire to mingle with someone of the opposite gender. This is normal, but it is only permitted in a marriage convent. And as parents, pastors, and mature adults, we must coach, mentor, and disciple our children and the younger generation with this profound truth, rather than shaming them with legalism and fear.

Just as our body serves a purpose in our lives and our spirit man serves a purpose as well, so does our sexuality. Our sexuality was not a mistake on God's part, nor was it a punishment or a cruel joke, but rather a blessing that is supposed to bring a married couple much pleasure, satisfaction, and fulfillment. And of course, through sexual intimacy, the husband can sow his seed into his wife, resulting in the birth of a new human being.

"KNOWING THAT YOU ARE A SEXUAL BEING SHOULD NOT EMBARRASS YOU, BUT RATHER GIVE YOU A BETTER UNDERSTANDING OF HOW YOUR HEAVENLY FATHER DESIGNED YOU TO BE."

THE FORBIDDEN "S" WORD

As I stated at the outset of this chapter, despite being born into a Christian family and raised in a church environment my entire life, I have never heard a biblical teaching or sound sermon about our sexuality. But I did hear a lot of sermons about sexual sins and how sex is a sin that were delivered with zeal. And when the Lord gave me the opportunity to serve as a youth pastor for about ten years, I did my best to address the topics of dating, relationships, and sexual purity, which occasionally got me in trouble with some church leadership and some complaints from parents. And the reason for this was that it seemed inappropriate to discuss such sensitive issues as sexuality and what the Bible had to say about it.

I remember once preaching at a Sunday service on the topic of Preserving and Protecting the Family Unit, and after the service, one of the pastors approached me and said, "Stan, you used some words today that I have never heard from the pulpit in all of my years in this local church." "Thank you very much!" This did not surprise me, but it was encouraging to hear that this pastor was grateful that I was brave enough to address such important issues in front of the congregation.

This so-called forbidden "S" word should not be forbidden, but rather embraced from a biblical perspective. As the body of Christ and as the local church, we must position ourselves to teach, preach, and talk about this "S" in a way that will give God's children hope, clarity, and sound biblical understanding. And as we do so, we will see many people who have the right kingdom mindset when it comes to what the Bible says about sex and our personal sexuality.

"INTIMACY IN MARRIAGE IS A GIFT FROM OUR HEAVENLY FATHER, AS WELL AS A FORM OF WORSHIP THAT BRINGS MUCH FULFILLMENT."

I DON'T UNTIL I DO

It will be difficult for an individual to say "no" when they need to or "yes" when they need to unless they have a degree of conviction towards something. This is also true when it comes to fully committing to remaining sexually pure until marriage. Later in the book, I'll share my personal testimony about being a virgin and how difficult it was for me to admit it boldly and openly to my high school classmates and friends.

So, what do I mean when I say: I don't until I do! This simply means that you will refrain from engaging in any sexual activity with the opposite gender. Regardless of how much you like each other or how deeply in love you are. And having sex is the highest level that any couple can achieve in any serious relationship and not kissing, hugging, or even touching sexual parts of the body. But the ultimate goal in these types of relationships is to have sex and establish yourself as a compatible pair.

And, while this may be the norm in the secular world, we as God's children must not follow these same destructive principles. And if you believe that you can control your sexual desires by only passionately kissing or embracing your boyfriend or girlfriend, you are highly mistaken. Many people, including those who considered themselves to be followers of Christ, have crossed the line in their dating or relationship, only to discover that they both ended up engaging in ungodly sexual behavior. As a result, some will simply brush off such deeds, while the majority will be haunted by guilt, shame, and condemnation.

I'm grateful that the living Word of God will always come to our aid, as we can see from some encouraging words written by King Solomon in the Songs of Solomon: "Daughters of Jerusalem, I charge you: Do not arouse or awaken love until it so desires."[2] This one-of-a-kind verse, which is used three times, emphasizes the importance of knowing our time and seasons and not allowing our feelings, emotions, or even sexual appetites to be aroused or awakened before the appropriate time. And this same verse in the Bible's love book should challenge anyone to make the bold decision to say, "I don't until I do!"

"STAYING SEXUALLY PURE IS NOT AN OUTDATED PRACTICE, BUT A COMMANDMENT FROM THE LORD."

RATED "R" RECOMMENDATIONS

- Because you are a sexual being, stop complaining about the natural attractions towards the opposite sex. Simply maintain self-control and walk in the fear of the Lord.
- The word sex, as well as discussions about our sexuality, should not be taboo in the body of Christ.
- Learn to use your willpower to say, "I don't until I do."
- Your sexuality is a gift from your Creator; therefore, do not treat it carelessly.
- Because you are a sexual being, allow the Holy Spirit to counsel and guide you until you marry, as He will teach you how to preserve your sexual purity.

3

SEXOLUTION

Sexolution! Stan, are you aware that this word does not even exist in the dictionary? Yes, and maybe someday it will! My purpose of incorporating this unique word was derived from the word *evolution*, which is defined as: change, expansion, progression, and transformation.[1]

And *sexolution* refers to the major shift that has occurred in our modern culture in terms of sex and sexuality. This evolution is altering how people perceive, interpret, and redefine the original true meaning of sexuality in relation to God's original purpose. And as a result of all of these drastic changes, we are witnessing a deadly transformation taking place in our culture, society, thinking, and the hearts and minds of the younger generation. And in this one-of-a-kind chapter, I'd like to sound some warning sirens to alert us to the deadly brainwashing that is viciously attacking our children and the younger generation.

ISN'T PORNOGRAPHY A FORM OF EDUCATION?

Absolutely no! Pornography is the absolute opposite to what the Word of God teaches us about sex and our sexuality. The word *pornography* is derived from the Greek *porni* ("prostitute") and *graphein* ("to write").[2] Pornography is frequently referred to as porn. This is truly amazing! As a result, whenever someone exposes themselves or indulges in porn, they are exposing themselves to a prostitute. This alone should serve as a wake-up call.

Furthermore, the entire purpose of pornography is to arouse and provide sexual pleasure to those who read erotic content, view photographic images, or watch the visual acts. Pornography also encourages both men and women to engage in personal masturbation in order to gain temporary satisfaction. Here are some sobering facts about the pornography industry:

<u>**Pornography Facts And Statistics**</u>

- *Global revenue of the porn industry is estimated around $90 billion.[3]*
- *Every second more than 28,000 users are watching porn on the internet.[4]*
- *Every day 37 pornographic videos are created in the USA.[5]*
- *Every day 2.5 billion emails containing porn are sent or received.[6]*
- *In 2019 one main porn website had 6.8 million new videos uploaded.[7]*
- *This same website in 2019 had more than 42 billion visits.[8]*

Years ago, I saw an eye-opening documentary about pornography and strip clubs. And one of the psychologists in the video made this astounding analysis over the years when he stated that while we are able to help people with various addictions, they have yet to discover a pill or specific treatment that could help someone break free from a porn addiction. Wow!

To say that pornography is a good form of education is akin to building a bong fire in the middle of a frozen lake and setting up a picnic table with your family. Porn is lethal, dangerous, and carries long-term destructive power that only Jesus' power and blood can break. And some may mistakenly believe that once they marry, they can allow porn into their marriage because the couple may get some ideas or even become aroused, which will eventually lead to intimacy. This is not only dangerous, but I have overheard some Christian couples do it on a regular basis. Again, sexual intimacy is only permitted within the marriage covenant, and it is also kept a closely guarded secret between the husband and wife, with no sharing of your intimate bedroom stories with friends or close siblings.

"LUST IS AN UNQUENCHABLE FIRE THAT WILL NEVER BE SATISFIED UNTIL IT HAS FULLY ACCOMPLISHED ITS PURPOSE."

ARE YOU SURE GOD CREATED YOU THIS WAY?

To answer the above question, we once again need to go to the original source, the Word, which says: "So God created man in His *own* image; in the image of God He created him; male and female He created them."[9] This passage clearly distinguishes only two genders: male and female. And for any professed Christian to see it any other way is to deny the Bible's authenticity and credibility.

And, in order to understand why there is so much confusion in our current culture regarding sexuality, we must return to the Garden of Eden. The serpent posed a question to Eve in the Garden of Eden: "Has God indeed said, 'You shall not eat of every tree in the garden'?"[10] This similar demonic question is still carving away at the hearts and minds on every human being as the enemy of our soul is saying:

- *Are you sure God created you this way?*
- *Are you sure you are a male?*
- *Are you sure you are a female?*
- *Are you sure that you only need to be attracted to the opposite sex?*
- *Are you sure that marriage will bring you happiness?*
- *Are you sure that you need to stay a virgin before you get married?*
- *Are you sure that you do not need any experience in dating or in having sex with someone to know if you two are compatible?*
- *Are you sure no one will make fun of you if they learn that you are still a virgin?*

This current *sexolution*, which is spreading rapidly, is confusing the hearts and minds of millions upon millions of people, particularly the younger generation. In my book, *Pathetic or Proactive Christianity*, I go into great detail about this topic. And, in light of the constant bombardment of messages aimed at our children's and youth's hearts and minds, it is critical for parents and the body of Christ to discuss our sexuality and what the Word of God says about us as God's perfect and divinely created masterpiece.

When our heavenly Father was forming you and me in our mother's womb, He didn't make a mistake about your gender or appearance. And God doesn't mess around with our sexuality or our kingdom identity. And in one of his Psalms, King David had something to say about this: "Oh yes, you shaped me first inside, then out; you formed me in my mother's womb."[11] I particularly like the Message translation of this verse because it emphasizes how our Heavenly Father has personally formed us both inwardly and outwardly.

"GOD NEVER MAKES MISTAKES. WHATEVER HIS HANDS CREATE, IT WILL BE A MASTERPIECE."

THIS IS MY BODY AND I CAN DO WHAT I WANT WITH IT!

Selfishness, self-centeredness, and demanding personal rights have reached new heights in our modern culture. And the common cry, from both men and women, is: This is my body, and I can do whatever I want with it! Yes, you have complete control over your body and can do whatever your heart or selfishness desires, but if you are a true born-again child of God, you understand that your body does not belong to you, but to the Lord, as Apostle Paul clearly stated: "Or do you not know that your body is the temple of the Holy Spirit who is in you, whom you have from God, and you are not your own? For you were bought at a price; therefore glorify God in your body and in your spirit, which are God's."[12]

The above passage makes it abundantly clear that our physical bodies, like the temple, are for the Holy Spirit to dwell in. Furthermore, Jesus paid a high price on the cross, by redeeming us from destruction. As a result of these, we must live in such a way that we bring glory to God through our bodies and our inner spirit man. And if the Bible describes our body as the temple of the Holy Spirit, then we must live a holy lifestyle, because darkness and light have nothing in common, and sexual immorality cannot coexist with the Holy Spirit.

When you and I grasp this powerful truth that our bodies do not belong to us, but to the Lord, we then begin to change our lifestyle, our daily habits, and submit our bodies to the guidance of the Holy Spirit who lives within us. Furthermore, if we choose to do what we want with our bodies rather than what the Holy Spirit wants, the consequences could be disastrous. And, arguably, sex and sexual pleasures are among the greatest fleshly appetites.

The wise King Solomon spent so much time teaching his sons about the dangers of lust and sexual appetites that he devoted three entire chapters in the Book of Proverbs to the subject. And the key factor here is that we must first recognize that our physical bodies are not ours, but the Lord's, and then learn to submit our bodies to His authority over our lives by submitting to the power of the Holy Spirit rather than the power of lust. Our bodies are made to bring glory and honor to God.

"THE BIBLE IS CLEAR IN STATING THAT OUR BODIES DO NOT BELONG TO US, BUT TO THE ONE WHO CREATED THEM."

GOD DID NOT MAKE A MISTAKE

It's mind-boggling to see how our society, academia, and social media are all fervently attempting to redefine everything we find in the Bible. Marriage, gender, morals, values, sexuality, and whether the baby in the womb is a human being or just a blob of tissues are all being redefined.

Furthermore, we should not succumb to the world's deceptive ideology, which is doing everything it can to erase what God originally said and re-define things in accordance with the demonic system. God, for example, created only two genders, male and female, and He did not leave the door open for the creation of additional genders. God created marriage as a union between a man and a woman, and God has clearly defined morals, values, and what is right and wrong.

And God did not make a mistake with you in all of His perfect creation. If you were born a male, this was God's original plan for your life. If you were born a female, it was God's perfect will for you to be a female in order to fulfill a specific purpose that a male cannot. However, whenever someone changes their gender or experiences same-sex attraction, they sincerely believe that is how they were created, and this same demonic belief has already crept into the body of Christ.

God is divine and perfect in every way, and it is with these same qualities that He created you and me, and we are not a mistake. We are His work of art! This is also true for marriage between a man and a woman, which has been perfectly designed to procreate and fill this earth with new life. As each child in the womb is a gift from above and possesses a kingdom purpose.

"GOD IS A DIVINE AND PERFECT GOD WHO ONLY CREATES MASTERPIECES. AND YOU ARE THAT WORK OF ART."

RATED "R" RECOMMENDATIONS

- Pornography, or any form of pornographic content, should be avoided because it will pervert your heart, mind, and perception of what sexuality is meant to be by God.
- You were created as a divine and flawless work of art. So, don't let the outside world define you.
- Your physical body was given to you to glorify your God and Creator, not to do whatever you want with it.
- God does not make any mistakes. Period!
- Discipline yourself to tune out the sexually perverted voices all around you.

4

MOM AND DAD WHERE ARE YOU?

Being a parent is exciting, adventurous, and exhausting. And in today's chaotic world, parenting can be difficult, with the temptation to abdicate our parental responsibilities and delegate them to someone else. And, as much as your child may be surrounded by the best teachers, coaches, and friends, none of them will ever be able to replace you as the most qualified individual to influence your child. Furthermore, your child could be attending the best church, with phenomenal children's ministry or youth programs, and with overqualified pastors, but this will not replace you as their parent who is capable of dealing with life's difficult issues.

And in this chapter, I want to remind every parent that their God-given role is to be the parent that God originally intended. And remember, it was your decision to bring your child into this world, not theirs!

TOO MANY DANGEROUS SUBSTITUTES

We've all had a substitute teacher at some point in our lives when we were in school. Substitute teachers were usually great because they didn't teach anything but would give you a simple classroom assignment that took less than ten minutes and then you could do whatever you wanted. But, as much as any student might enjoy this time off, the following day, the regular classroom teacher would be back in charge. As a result, the primary function of any substitute is to temporarily fill in for the specifically designated teacher. Even if the substitute is only there for a week or two, they will not be able to teach in the same way as the original teacher, and it will take time for them to connect with the students.

When it comes to parenting, the same principle applies. We can do our best to have teachers, coaches, other parents, church leaders, or other adults fill in for the lazy parent by acting as a substitute parent in your child's life. And this is where the danger lies, because our children and the younger generation already have too many dangerous substitutes, such as social media, toxic friends, immoral legislation, unbiblical education in schools and colleges, and a plethora of socialistic teachers and professors with a hidden agenda.

"MOM AND DAD, YOU ARE YOUR CHILD'S BEST TOOL, RESOURCE, COACH, COUNSELOR, AND GUIDE. AND GOD HAS EQUIPPED YOU WITH ALL OF THE KNOWLEDGE AND WISDOM YOU REQUIRE."

THE NUMBER ONE SOURCE

The day you decided to have a child was the day you became the primary source of discipline, nurturing, and raising your child in accordance with the living Word of God. And, yes, your heavenly Father has already equipped you to instill kingdom and biblical principles in your child's life. Sure, you may not feel adequate, experienced, or even knowledgeable about life, but that should never be an excuse for you not fulfilling your parental role in your child's life.

With that said, the topics of dating, relationships, marriage, and sexuality have been placed on the shoulders of every parent who needs to talk with their child about these important topics. Of course, they must be of the appropriate age demographic. Now, if you, as a parent, choose to abdicate your parental responsibilities because a particular subject makes you uncomfortable, or if you simply choose to be ignorant about these matters, you are putting your child in jeopardy.

Right now, social media, various apps, friends, and Hollywood are the primary sources through which the youth are introduced to the concepts of dating, relationships, and sex. And the church is backpedaling its position, despite the fact that the church and the Word of God should be the primary sources. And as the body of Christ awakens from its spiritual slumber, we will be able to serve as a much-needed credible source for the younger generation.

Furthermore, every parent must seize the parental baton and position themselves as the most credible source to their child, but this cannot simply come from the parent alone; each and every parent must be fully connected with their Creator and continually draw the much-needed wisdom, knowledge, and revelation to how to raise and educate their child from the fundamental principles of the Word of God.

"GOD HAS GIVEN PARENTS THE RESPONSIBILITY OF BEING THE PRIMARY SOURCE OF INFORMATION, CONSULTATION, GUIDANCE, ENCOURAGEMENT, AND CLARIFICATION TO THEIR CHILD."

MOM AND DAD, DON'T BE IGNORANT!

I don't claim to have all the answers or even the most qualified experience as a parent but having served as a youth pastor for a number of years and now having two of my own teenagers has allowed me to observe patterns and specific symptoms as it relates to dating and relationships amongst the youth. I can count on my fingers all of those who dated in high school and eventually married, while the rest went through a handful of relationships, many of which ended bitterly, while others left a lasting trauma in the hearts and minds of the youth.

So, I suppose the reality check questions that must be raised are:

- *Is it necessary to have a certain number of boyfriends (girlfriends) before finding the right one who will eventually be their spouse?*

- *How many broken relationships does one have to go through before learning the valuable lesson of waiting for the mature time when they need to enter a potential serious relationship?*
- *What is the healthy accepted number of different boyfriends/girlfriends your child should have before deciding enough is enough?*

How comfortable should the parent be with the idea that someone (boyfriend/girlfriend) may be inappropriately caressing your child or doing things they are not supposed to be doing behind your back?

All of the preceding may appear to be common sense, but it is this common sense that appears to be lacking in the body of Christ. And over the years, I've seen how parents, or often single mothers, simply turn a blind eye while the boyfriend is caressing their daughter during church service, or how both of them can't take their hands off each other. And this is common among many parents. Of course, some of you may take this out of context and conclude that I'm being too judgmental or spiritual, but this is far from the truth.

Any parent wants the best for their child, and any parent will go to any length to ensure that their son or daughter is happy. However, a common mistake that can be made in the process is believing that if my fifteen-year-old daughter has a boyfriend, she will be happy, or that if my sixteen-year-old son has a girlfriend, he will not feel lonely or depressed. This is a dangerous concept because these young and immature teens did not know how to create healthy boundaries in their relationships, which resulted in broken hearts, the girl becoming pregnant, depression, and numerous suicides. Yes, all the above are the result of teens being exposed to the world of dating and relationships at an early age.

Again, my above assessment may incite rage in some parents and youth, but there is a reason why we have specific laws in place to protect and guide us in life. Why does it seem illogical to deny a twelve-year-old driver silence? Why is it necessary to be a certain age to operate certain dangerous machinery? Alternatively, why are there certain high-paying jobs that will never hire a seventeen-year-old? This should be no different when it comes to encouraging and teaching our sons and daughters to only date when they are mature enough, or when they believe they are ready to enter into a serious relationship.

"AS LONG AS YOUR CHILD IS STILL LIVING WITH YOU, YOU HAVE COMPLETE CONTROL OVER WHAT YOU ALLOW AND WHAT YOU FORBID."

RATED "R" RECOMMENDATIONS

- Your parent (parents) is not your adversary. They are not without flaws, but they are God's instrument in your life.
- The Bible will always be the most reliable source for answers to your most difficult questions. So, consider this *Rated R* manual to be your best friend.

- Dear parents, please do not ignore the issues of dating, relationships, marriage preparation, and the importance of teaching your child to remain sexually pure.
- Please learn from your parents' negative or positive experiences when they were single, dating, or in various relationships.
- If you were born out of wedlock, please learn from your parent's mistakes and do not make the same one for your personal life.
- If you parents are currently divorced, again allow this to become a powerful teachable moment.
- As difficult as it may be at times, never substitute your parents with someone else who you believe has your best interests at heart.

5

DON'T WORRY JESUS WILL FORGIVE YOU

What great hope we have in the cross, the blood, and the forgiveness of our sins that only Jesus was able to provide for everyone. And the power of forgiveness is so incredible that our minds can only grasp a fraction of what it truly means. With that said, we've made it a habit to talk about forgiveness as if it were something you could pick up in a grocery store and pay for at the register. On the contrary, many so-called Christians have mocked and continue to mock Jesus' death and resurrection, as well as the power of His blood, by willfully sinning or watering down God's Word. And in this crucial chapter, I want to explain what a willful sin is, and why many people get caught up in the belief that "everyone is doing it," and how the law of sowing and reaping can help.

WHAT IS A WILLFUL SIN?

Sin is sin, no matter how you look at it, but there is a difference between committing a sinful deed because you were stressed, spiritually weak, let down your spiritual guard, or thought you were spiritually strong enough to walk away from the temptation, and committing a sinful deed because you know it is a sin and everything within you is screaming not to do it, but you still do it.

The writer of Hebrews expresses this truth bluntly: "For if we sin willfully after we have received the knowledge of the truth, there no longer remains a sacrifice for sins, but a certain fearful expectation of judgment, and fiery indignation which will devour the adversaries."[1] Furthermore, the dictionary defines *willful* as: someone who is headstrong, self-willed, and stiff-necked.[2] Again, to commit a willful sin, you must be fully aware that what you are about to do is wrong, and the Holy Spirit who lives within you is screaming loud and clear for you not to do it.

Finally, it has almost become a new trend among Christians to do whatever they want, fully aware that it is wrong, only to later go and repent. Some refer to this as God's never-ending grace, while others proclaim, "God is all loving and all forgiving!" That is correct, but God is also accountable to His own Word, which He cannot and will not contradict.

Furthermore, another toxic belief that is wreaking havoc on the Christian community is the notion that as long as we do not murder anyone or commit a heinous criminal act, we can always return to the Lord and ask for His mercy, forgiveness and grace. This, once again, is a deception from the pits of hell. It is one thing to be born into a non-Christian family, but it is quite another to be born into a Christian family or surrounded by

Christian folks and have heard enough of the truth of God's Word, and then this same individual decides to live a loose life, believing that there will be no consequences.

Yes, there will be consequences, and sometimes they will be bitterly painful, as the Word of God has outlined that if you willfully sin, you count the sacrifice and blood of Jesus of no value or importance, which voids its power to work in your personal life, and as a result, God's discipline and punishment comes into play. This is something that Christian folks do not want to discuss or think about because it will make many people uncomfortable and portray our Christian faith as unloving or cruel.

"YOUR WILLFUL CHOICES TODAY WILL SHAPE YOUR TOMORROW AND EVEN YOUR FUTURE."

EVERYBODY IS DOING IT!

As carnal beings, it is all too easy for us to get caught up in the attitude of: Everyone else is doing it! So why shouldn't I? And this mindset is often much more prevalent among the younger generation, particularly among middle school, high school, and college students. They would naturally want to replicate what their peers and friends are doing or what many are talking about. And the mentality that says, "Well, most of my friends have girlfriends, so why shouldn't I?" Or being sexually active appears to be normal because it is so cool!

Yes, everyone else is free to do whatever they want, but we, as God's children, must say "no" where "no" is required and choose a lifestyle of holiness, purity, and righteousness. Yes, this can be difficult at times, but the wise Apostle Paul offers us hope and clarity when he says: "Therefore, if anyone *is* in Christ, *he is* a new creation; old things have passed away; behold, all things have become new."[3] And the main takeaway is that we are a new creation in Christ, and that our old sinful nature has died. But, with that said, Apostle Paul makes a clarification by saying, "If anyone is in Christ," which means he is challenging you and me to examine our hearts to ensure that we are in Christ.

And those who truly are in Christ have and continue to crucify their carnal nature and appetites to the cross, and in doing so, they should not be concerned with doing what the world is doing or becoming entangled with the sinful nature of this world, as many others do. No, the children of God do not do what the children of the devil do, and today, my friend, you must make that bold distinction as to whether you are a child of God or not, and if you are, you are a new creation, and as a new creation, you automatically have a new nature, which is Christ, who is holy and righteous.

"DO NOT SUCCUMB TO A SHEEP MENTALITY BY FOLLOWING THE HERD THAT IS ABOUT TO FALL OFF THE CLIFF."

SOWING AND REAPING IS A LAW

The law of sowing and reaping is a real law, not a cute biblical illustration. What you sow is what you will reap. But wait, Jesus atoned for my sin! Yes, He did, but this does not automatically nullify the law of sowing and reaping; otherwise, the Word of God loses credibility. So, what does all of this mean? Sowing and reaping functions as a law enforcement officer, where if you are not breaking the law and are doing everything legally, you should not be afraid of the officer, but if you are breaking the law, you should be uncomfortable and fearful of being arrested.

This principle also holds true when it comes to sin. Committing a sinful act is breaking God's law or going against His divine Word, but if you are not committing or living in sin, the law of God has no power to judge you, as Apostle Paul stated: "Therefore do not let sin reign in your mortal body, that you should obey it in its lusts. And do not present your members as instruments of unrighteousness to sin, but present yourselves to God as being alive from the dead, and your members as instruments of righteousness to God. For sin shall not have dominion over you, for you are not under law but under grace."[4]

Sowing and reaping is a biblical principle, and the apostle Paul instructs us not to allow sin to reign in our bodies, but rather to present our entire body to the Lord, so that our physical body can become an instrument for God's purpose on this earth. And, as I previously stated, sexual immorality is the most serious sin or damage to your body, and we as God's children should not be fooled into thinking that we can do whatever we want because there will be no consequences. Submit your body to your heavenly Father's loving care and watch what He does in and through you.

"SOW GOOD SEEDS INTO YOUR LIFE WHILE YOU ARE STILL SINGLE, SO THAT WHEN YOU MARRY, YOU CAN REAP THE MUCH-NEEDED BLESSINGS AND REWARDS."

RATED "R" RECOMMENDATIONS

- Yes, Jesus will forgive you, but this does not and should not give you permission to sin.
- You can still be forgiven for a willful sin, but you don't want to risk the dire consequences of such sinful actions.
- Sowing and reaping is a divine law, not a suggestion, thought, or a side note.
- Being different is not shameful but participating in what the rest of the world is doing, does not make you cool.
- Jesus loves you and will forgive your sins, but don't take advantage of this divine privilege, because sins have a significant cost.
- If you have a particular sin that is constantly oppressing you, make the courageous decision to bring it to the feet of Jesus, who is capable of giving you victory.

6

SOUL TIES

What exactly are soul ties? A soul tie is a spiritual or emotional connection to a specific individual that often occurs after having intimate sexual relations with them. As a result, you form an emotional bond with that person. This emotional bond functions similarly to coding, programming your thoughts, feelings, desires, and inner soul.

Soul ties in marriage are strong because they are based on the divine covenant made between the man and the woman on their first wedding night. However, soul ties formed outside of a married covenant can have disastrous consequences, such as:

- Control
- Manipulation
- Fear and Anxiety
- Stress
- Distrust
- Insecurity

The truth about soul ties is that the more sex partners you have in your life, the more soul ties you will have. And the longer you live this way, the stronger these soul ties will become. In a nutshell, soul ties are frequently accompanied by demons and demonic oppression. This is a bold statement, but when you are not under a biblical covenant, you open yourself up to the spiritual realm, and the demons that stand behind sexual immorality are dark and brutal.

Furthermore, as Apostle Paul powerfully stated that if you sexually unite yourself with a prostitute, then "Two will become one flesh."[1] What exactly does this mean? For example, if you mix one rotten egg with one good egg and make an omelet, you will still smell the rotten egg and the omelet will taste bad. Or, if you simply mix one tiny drop of poison into a gallon of water and then drink it, you will most likely become very ill or die. Again, if you mix white and black paints, you will get a grey color where the white and black paints have lost their originality.

This principle also applies to soul ties. When two people have a sexual intercourse, they merge into one. Two bodies merge to form one. Two spirits merge to form one. Two souls merge to form one. And whatever garbage or baggage each individual is carrying in their personal life, such as sin, additions, lust, or demons, can be attached to the other person. You see, you don't have to smoke, but if you're in the same room as someone who does, you'll start to smell like cigarette smoke. And if you are constantly around people who smoke, you are exposed to what is known as secondhand smoke. And, as a result of their research and study, the CDC stated: "Secondhand smoke contains more than 7,000 chemicals. Hundreds are toxic and seventy can cause cancer. And since 1964 Surgeon General's Report, 2.5 million adults who were nonsmokers died because they breathed secondhand smoke."[2]

Furthermore, soul ties act as superglue. When you use superglue to hold something together, it will be extremely difficult and time-consuming to separate. Much strength, time, and energy will be expended in this process, but you can be certain that whatever you are attempting to separate from the superglue will not look the same, and there is also a good chance that you will break or damage whatever you are attempting to separate. The same principle applies here. Even if you end a relationship or have a one-night stand, you are still bound to that person, whether you like it or not. And in this chapter, I'll delve deep into this critical issue in order to shed some light on the corrosive bondage of soul ties.

YOUR PAST MEMORIES WILL FOLLOW YOU FOR THE REST OF YOUR LIFE

Without a doubt, the blood of Jesus has the power to forgive you and wash away all your sins. With that said, why does the enemy of our soul show us flashbacks to our sinful deeds in the past? Why does a perverse or lustful thought, or even a sexual image or movie scene from many years ago, appear out of nowhere in your mind? It makes no difference how spiritual you are, how much you pray, read the Bible, or even fast; the serpent of old will attack our previous thoughts and memories at any given opportunity in order to divert us or lure us back into our sinful past.

Why should you avoid sex before marriage? Why should you keep your eyes untainted by pornographic images or sex scenes? And why should you refrain from engaging in any perverse or promiscuous behavior? So, you will have no bad memories! Your brain, you see, is similar to a computer hard drive in that it can store an infinite amount of information. And all of our previous memories, whether positive or negative, are saved in our memory bank. And some of those thoughts will come to you when you least expect it.

And these memories can manifest as still images, play out as a short video clip, or even elicit a feeling or emotional response within us. Again, the power of Jesus' blood can deliver anyone from being haunted or oppressed by thoughts of previous mistakes made, but the memories do not simply vanish. And Apostle Paul gives us sound advice when he says: "And do not be conformed to this world, but be transformed by the renewing of your mind, that you may prove what *is* that good and acceptable and perfect will of God."[3]

The key recommendation is that we constantly renew our minds and submit them to God's will. And as you continually submit your life to God's will and allow your heart and mind to be attached to Him, you will strengthen your bond with the lover of your soul and will not allow your soul to become attached to another soul that does not belong in your life.

> ## "EVERY ACTION, DEED OR WORD GETS PERMANENTLY STORED INTO YOUR MEMORY BANK. AND SOONER OR LATER YOU WILL MAKE WITHDRAWALS."

TWO SHALL BECOME ONE

The Bible is truly amazing because it covers every aspect of life, including sexual intimacy, and in the gospel of Mark, we find this profound passage that reads: "For this reason a man shall leave his father and mother and be joined to his wife, and the two shall become one flesh' so then they are no longer two, but one flesh."[4]

And Apostle Paul also addresses this same point in 1 Corinthians 6:16.

What does this imply? God originally intended that when a man and a woman in a marriage covenant engage in sexual intimacy, they both become like one body, just as those who are born-again are joined together in one body with Christ. This is a powerful truth to grasp: just as we become one with Christ, the husband and wife become one flesh. But, as I mentioned at the start of this chapter, any time and every time two people engage in sexual intercourse, they both become one. The crucial question is, one with what or who?

Two becoming one is a divine principle, and in marriage, this principle is honored by our heavenly Father, who takes great delight and satisfaction when His children join together in intimacy, which is one of the blessings that a married couple receives under the marriage covenant.

"TWO BECOMING ONE IS A POWERFUL UNION THAT ORIGINATED IN HEAVEN." AND THIS BOND IS SUPPORTED BY GOD HIMSELF."

THE GREATEST SIN AGAINST YOUR OWN BODY

The great Apostle Paul says something very bold about sexual immorality: "Flee sexual immorality. Every sin that a man does is outside the body, but he who commits sexual immorality sins against his own body."[5] This is the only verse in the Bible that explicitly states that sexual immorality has a negative impact on your physical body. And it should come as no surprise that sexual illnesses, diseases, and viruses are among the most painful and lethal to the human body. Sexual sin manifests itself in a person's physical body.

Furthermore, King Solomon goes into great detail with his sons about the destruction that awaits you if you yield yourself to an adulterous woman. Let's take a close look at this passage:

> [1] My son, pay attention to my wisdom;
> listen carefully to my wise counsel.
> [2] Then you will show discernment,
> and your lips will express what you've learned.
> [3] For the lips of an immoral woman are as sweet as honey,
> and her mouth is smoother than oil.
> [4] But in the end she is as bitter as poison,
> as dangerous as a double-edged sword.
> [5] Her feet go down to death;
> her steps lead straight to the grave.
> [6] For she cares nothing about the path to life.
> She staggers down a crooked trail and doesn't realize it.
> [7] So now, my sons, listen to me.
> Never stray from what I am about to say:
> [8] Stay away from her!
> Don't go near the door of her house!
> [9] If you do, you will lose your honor
> and will lose to merciless people all you have achieved.
> [10] Strangers will consume your wealth,
> and someone else will enjoy the fruit of your labor.
> [11] In the end you will groan in anguish
> when disease consumes your body.
> -Proverbs 5:1-11

Let us now dive deep into the powerful insight and warning that some of the preceding verses address:

- V – 3 *Sexual appetites will always appear to be as sweet as honey on the outside.*
- V – 4 *Once you have succumbed to sexual immorality, you will be on a deadly path of destruction.*
- V – 6 *Sexual sins deal the most severe blows to your life, body, and future, as their ultimate goal is to destroy you.*
- V – 9 *"Lose your honor" is referring to losing your sexual purity (virginity).*
- V – 10 *Who are these strangers who will indulge in the fruits of your labor? This passage is about divorce caused by adultery or unfaithfulness in marriage. And, after a divorce, another man (future husband or boyfriend) will typically live in your home with your ex-wife, enjoying what you previously worked for.*
- V – 11 *A powerful warning about various sexual diseases (HIV/AIDS, HPV, Herpes, Syphilis, Gonorrhea, Chlamydia).*

This should send shivers down your spine because the Word of God addresses every aspect of life if we only choose to understand God's blessings as well as His dire warnings. And, as I close this breathtaking chapter, I want to encourage you that if you have made selfish mistakes in the area of sexuality, your heavenly Father is eager to forgive you and give you a fresh start if you will allow Him to. And I want to challenge you to make a firm decision to live a life of purity and holiness, because doing so will bring many blessings into your life as a single person or into your marriage.

"YOU CAN ALWAYS BE FORGIVEN FOR YOUR SINS, BUT THE CONSEQUENCES WILL NOT SIMPLY VANISH."

RATED "R" RECOMMENDATIONS

- If the prospect of having your past memories follow you for the rest of your life scares you, then make only positive memories.
- Always remember that any form of sexual intimacy or intercourse unites two people into one flesh.
- Sexual sins can lead to deadly diseases like HIV, so don't put yourself in a position where you think you'll be immune to such a dreadful disease.
- Before entering into a serious relationship or engaging in sexual behavior, soul ties are probably the last thing on anyone's mind. From now on, be aware of the destructive strongholds of soul ties.
- Make today the day you start making good memories that will last the rest of your life.

7

IN SOCIAL MEDIA I TRUST

If you look closely at any US currency, you will notice a written statement that says, "In God we trust." This is, without a doubt, a daring declaration, which many have attempted to obliterate permanently. And, while many people have made money their God, there is a new competitor on the horizon: social media.

With the rise of the social media empire, it's no surprise that Christian folks and youth are putting a lot of faith in the content that's being shared on these platforms. It will also come as no surprise to anyone, especially parents, that our children get a lot of their information, knowledge, and answers from these various social media platforms. But the crucial reality check question is: What kind of answers are they getting to their most pressing life questions? And in this chapter, I wanted to highlight some of the most popular and influential social media platforms that have evolved into universities, the new ten commandments, new role models, and a new perspective on what love should be.

THE UNIVERSITY OF YOUTUBE

I'm grateful to YouTube for allowing me to discover and obtain a wealth of knowledge, wisdom, truth, and insight related to my personal and spiritual development. And I've also seen and heard a lot of content that was perplexing, strange, and extremely dangerous.

I would not be mistaken if I labeled YouTube as a type of university capable of both educating and brainwashing others, as many liberal and atheistic professors are currently doing on college campuses. And I'd like to challenge you, my friend, to exercise great caution when it comes to what content, teaching, or information you allow yourself to consume, particularly when it comes to dating, relationships, marriages, or sex. And I don't mean wrong theological teachers and pastors, but rather so-called relationship and sex experts who have already been divorced, have no children, or live a sexually promiscuous lifestyle, but do have their own YouTube channel with thousands of subscribers and millions of views.

"KNOWLEDGE IS POWER, BUT NOT ALL KNOWLEDGE OR INFORMATION IS BENEFICIAL, SO BE WATCHFUL ABOUT WHO YOU ALLOW TO BE YOUR TEACHER."

THE TEN COMMANDMENTS OF INSTAGRAM

For a while, my wife and two teenage children would tell me that I needed to get an Instagram account because everyone else was using it. I eventually did, probably because I was already being mocked by my two teenagers for being out of touch by not being on the platform where most others are currently active.

Instagram hasn't been particularly noteworthy for me, but it does have its own distinct personality. So, why do I refer to Instagram as the "ten commandments"? To begin, let us examine the word Instagram to gain a better understanding of the origins of the creative and catchy social media name. Instagram is made up of two words: *insta*, which comes from the word instant or instantly. And the word *gram*, is a metric unit that measures mass or weight. And it also signifies something that is written down or recorded like a telegram.[1]

So, in a nutshell, Instagram is a platform where you can instantly and quickly share your thoughts, feelings, images, or a part of your life with a group or a mass of people who can then comment, react, or weigh in with their personal opinions. Again, this is a great and convenient platform for keeping your circle of friends, family members, or connections up to date on what is going on in your personal life, and it does make our world a much smaller place.

Having said that, a platform like Instagram has the potential to overexpose you to unhealthy posts, stories, or reels that could pollute your eyes, mind, and subconscious. Because we have such ease in quickly sharing our thoughts or images from our daily lives, this same advantage of doing whatever we want opens the door for us all to be instantly exposed to unhealthy, dangerous, and even demonic contents that are easily accessible with a swipe of our finger.

Again, why the ten commandments of Instagram? Instagram has no limits or boundaries, and it allows you easy access to people you don't know or will never meet in person, but you can follow them and their content, whether good or misleading. And some of the content posted does serve as commandments, educating you and suggesting that this type of behavior or lifestyle is great, or giving you tips and suggestions on how to seduce a girl, or sharing insight into how many different sex positions you could experiment with your partner. And the list could go on and on.

"THERE IS A MASSIVE INFLUX OF SUGGESTIONS, RECOMMENDATIONS, AND MAN'S PERSONAL OPINIONS, BUT THERE ARE ONLY TEN ORIGINAL COMMANDMENTS."

THE WORLDWIDE ROLE MODEL CALLED TIKTOK

As I write this, TikTok has over 1 billion monthly users, and in 2020 they generated a revenue of $1.9 billion dollars. And out of roughly 4.8 billion internet users worldwide, about 20.8% use TikTok.[2] Those are mind-boggling figures to grasp. And I'm confident that these figures will continue to rise.

Personally, I am not on TikTok and am not a fan of this social media platform. There are advantages and disadvantages to everything but based on my experience with my two teenagers and the research I have done, I have concluded that TikTok is extremely toxic and dangerous.

TikTok, in a nutshell, is a video-focused social media craze that provides its users with limitless opportunities to create short video clips using their infinite creativity. These short videos could be funny, very creative, and entertaining, with a variety of genres such as pranks, stunts, challenges, and dance moves. And some of these short clips are so unique or creative that they go viral, generating millions of views in a matter of days.

Without a doubt TikTok has captivated the hearts and minds of the younger generation who are anxiously looking forward to becoming popular, famous, recognizable, and known all over the world simply because one of their videos went viral and or even made it on the national news. Again, this instant fame or exposure comes with a poisonous bite in that many of these teenagers are unable to cope or handle the expedited fame or popularity that quickly enters their heads, and as a result, these same individuals lay down their guard, throw off restraint, and become extremely vulnerable. This vulnerability frequently leads to depression, substance abuse, and even suicide.

Isn't that a bit of an exaggeration on your part, Stan? Not at all! As a parent of two teenagers and having had the opportunity to spend quality time with teenagers, I have seen and continue to see how social media, particularly TikTok, is brainwashing the younger generation. And once a monetary influx enters a young teenager's life, both fame and money overtake the innocent and immature minds of these teenagers, who become rebellious at home and expose themselves to perverse or sexually immoral lifestyles.

I've seen my fair share of some of the most popular videos or TikTokers who record themselves in bikinis, or show way too much cleavage, or have positioned themselves in an erotic posture while video recording themselves. Again, TikTok does not have to be a dangerous platform, but the power of its influence is uncontrollable, and if you as a Christian do not set Godly boundaries for yourself, you will become vulnerable to falling deep into the traps of TikTok or any other popular social media platforms.

TikTok has emerged as the new role model to which the majority of its users are submitting. A role model, once again, is someone or something who serves as an example, a mentor, a hero, an idol, or a superstar. And many aspire to be the next idol or superstar to whom millions of followers will look up. And this same platform has already done a lot of damage in terms of what dating is, as well as a lot of toxic exposure to sexually immoral behaviors, lifestyles, and recommendations.

"SEEK OUT ROLE MODELS WHO ARE GENUINELY CONCERNED WITH YOUR SUCCESS AND WELL-BEING."

THE LOVE STORIES OF AMAZON PRIME, NETFLIX, HBO, HULU, AND DISNEY PLUS

As someone who enjoys watching good movies and captivating TV shows, I am always on the lookout for new releases, which often seem catchy during their two-minute trailer, but in recent years I have been very disappointed as I would start a brand-new TV series only to discover how saturated it is with the LGBTQ agenda, and nonstop sexual promiscuity.

Movies that were previously labelled as rated R due to sexual scenes or obscene language are now rated as PG-13. And, with the rapid proliferation of new streaming services, nearly all of them are on the same perverse page. Even the devoted Hallmark channel, which featured some of the best family movies and Christmas specials, has recently joined the LGBTQxyz club.

Do we have to stop watching or subscribing to these streaming networks as a result of this? No, and, as with anything else, we must use discernment and common sense. This also applies to any other social media platform. Yes, you can uninstall any social media app that you believe is harmful, but you can also exercise your free will in the process.

My sincere and heartfelt recommendation is that if you believe or notice that a specific app, social media platform, or streaming network is capturing much of your valuable time, or is exposing you to sexually immoral content, or is causing much confusion as it relates to your identity, gender, or Christian beliefs, then uninstall or unsubscribe.

"ENTERTAINMENT IS NOT A SIN BUT USE GODLY DISCERNMENT IN CHOOSING THE TYPE OF CONTENT YOU CONSUME."

DO NOT TRY TO FIX WHAT IS NOT BROKEN

It's easy to get caught up in all the presumably beneficial aspects of the social media revolution, with seemingly limitless information at our fingertips. And with such limitless power and potential, we can become entrapped into relying on these social media platforms as our primary source of information, neglecting the supreme Source, which is God's Word.

God's Word is not broken! It is not outdated! And we shouldn't try to fix something that isn't broken. Marriages are in shambles. Relationships are shattered and torn apart. Hearts are broken bitterly. Children are frequently the victims of broken families. And we live in a broken society that is confused and delusional when it comes to understanding what dating should be, the purpose of sexual purity, and the significance of a marriage covenant.

And because the Word of God has been tested and endured over time and generations, it has earned the reputation that it deserves, and we as parents, church leaders, and Godly role models must direct our children, the younger generation, and married couples to the original Source, and boldly declare: In God we trust!

> "THE TRUTH AND POWER OF GOD'S WORD ARE THE ONLY THINGS THAT CAN REPAIR THE BROKENNESS OF THIS WORLD."

RATED "R" RECOMMENDATIONS

- As you browse your preferred social media platform, remember to use discernment and wisdom in what you allow into your mind and heart.
- Always remember that the eyes are the lamp to your inner soul.
- Because visual or still images become embedded in your subconscious, so utilize much discretion to what you allow to become programmed into your memory bank.
- God's Word is not broken or out of date; it is and always will be the most up-to-date source of information available.
- Allow the Bible to become your go-to app.
- Allow the living Word of God to serve as your filter, filtering out all of the garbage that is thrown at you.

8

I AM STILL A VIRGIN!

The term "virgin" is all too familiar to the average Christian, who is at least familiar with the Word of God in relation to the Virgin Mary, who conceived Christ without knowing any man intimately. And the story of Mary, Jesus' mother, is well-known throughout the world, particularly during the Christmas season. Furthermore, it appears intriguing that an adult can easily dismiss the true meaning of why Mary is often referred to as Virgin Mary, particularly among Catholics, but not everyone would focus on the fact that she was a virgin when she conceived Christ. This is a critical point to understand!

The almighty God did not choose Mary at random because she was more special; He chose her because Mary had a pure heart and was also a virgin. This profound truth must not be overlooked. And in this fascinating chapter, I want to discuss the importance of sexual purity, share my personal testimony, and offer hope to those who have made foolish mistakes in their lives and are no longer virgins.

WHAT IS SEXUAL PURITY?

Sexual purity is when you make the courageous decision not to get involved or take part in any type of sexual behavior with the opposite gender in order to keep your virginity until you marry. And sexual purity entails not only not having sexual relations with others, but also protecting your heart, mind, and eyes from pornography and sexually immoral people.

Again, we can glean another powerful piece of advice from Apostle Paul in his letter to Timothy, his young protégé, as he stated: "Don't let anyone think less of you because you are young. Be an example to all believers in what you say, in the way you live, in your love, your faith, and your purity."[1] In this passage, Apostle Paul encouraged Timothy while also challenging him to set a good example for other believers in the area of *purity*.

This is an important insight because Timothy was a powerful leader in the body of Christ, and Apostle Paul was challenging him to be a credible role model for others who looked up to him. So, sexual purity is a recommendation to all believers in Christ, not just a holy encryption engraved on the foreheads of righteous individuals. Being sexually pure is a blessing to you and will become a blessing to others because the Lord will be able to use you as a pure vessel, just like Virgin Mary, to bless others.

And I vividly recall one conversation with a coworker with whom I worked when I was engaged. When I told her I was still a virgin, she laughed in disbelief. But after I shared my personal testimony with her, she later that day approached me with a sad countenance and told me that she is jealous of me because I was able to keep my virginity for my bride-to-be and that both of us were getting married as virgins. She went on to say that she wished she could have made the same good decisions in her own life.

"KEEPING YOURSELF PURE BEFORE MARRYING WILL RESULT IN A STRONGER AND MORE SPECIAL BOND WITH YOUR FUTURE SPOUSE."

I AM STILL A VIRGIN!

Taking on the vital importance of virginity, or why it is so important for every child of God to marry as virgins, as this is a Biblical commandment that comes with many blessings. And the Book of Proverbs uses this powerful illustration to discuss sexual purity: "Drink water from your own well – share your love only with your wife. Why spill the water of your springs in the streets, having sex with just anyone? You should reserve it for yourself. Never share it with stranger. Let your wife be a fountain of blessing for you. Rejoice in the wife of your youth."[2]

The key takeaways are primarily about sexual purity and only embracing yourself in sexual intimacy with your spouse, and King Solomon takes a unique approach to referencing our virginity to *water* and challenging everyone to drink water from our own *well,* and this well is symbolic of the marriage covenant between the husband and the wife. Furthermore, Solomon challenges us not to share our water (sexual intimacy) with anyone other than our spouse. "Rejoice in the wife of your youth," he said as his final words. That is the main point here: sexual intimacy with your spouse is a great pleasure.

Allow me to share my personal testimony. I was very athletic with a strong built body when I was in high school back in the 1920's (just kidding), and as much as it would be strange for me to be complimenting myself on my good looks, I knew that a handful of girls were very interested in me, but I had an inner fear of dating anyone. As time passed, my friends and some of my popular classmates began to ask, "Stan, why don't you have a girlfriend?" Or say, "Are you gay?" Or the most dreadful of all questions: "Stan, are you still a virgin?"

After a while, these types of questions began to bother me, as I felt like the black sheep, knowing that I could have a girlfriend and become sexually active like many of my classmates, but there was this inner fear, which I believe was the result of my parents' endless prayers for me. Anyway, over time, I developed a defense mechanism to get my friends and classmates off my back by saying, "No, I'm not a virgin!" Or make up some ridiculous story about what I and this girl did this past weekend just to appear cool and relevant to my peers. Of course, this was before I knew the Lord and Jesus was not the center of my life. But when the Holy Spirit took hold of me, my answers to these same questions changed.

And as time passed, I began to boldly share with others why I was still a virgin, and yes, many laughed, some were convinced I was lying, and others commended me on my strong inner convictions. And I remember telling someone during one of our conversations that I wholeheartedly believed my future wife would also be a virgin, and again, some laughed, some said, "Yeah right!" and some agreed with me.

Finally, on June 1st, 2002, I married the love of my life, and yes, we were both virgins on our first bridal night. And my personal testimony is not meant to brag or to rub it in someone's face, but simply to say that yes, it is possible to preserve your virginity before marriage with the help of the Holy Spirit and God's hand over your life, but you must make that strong decision right now to surrender yourself and your body into the arms of your heavenly Father, so He can give you the strength, boldness, and wisdom to live out your singleness days. And, yes, when someone asks you, "Are you still a virgin?" "Yes, I am still a virgin," you will confidently respond.

"YOU MAY NOT BE COOL OR POPULAR RIGHT NOW BECAUSE YOU CHOOSE TO REMAIN SEXUALLY PURE, BUT THE FUTURE BLESSINGS WILL ALWAYS BE WORTH IT."

THE FIRST BRIDAL NIGHT SHOULD BE HOLY AND SACRED

As I mentioned in my personal testimony about my wife and I marrying as virgins, our first bridal night was sacred and holy, and it hasn't changed to this day. So, what makes the first bridal night holy and sacred in our heavenly Father's eyes? To uncover this sacred truth, we must first return to the Old Testament, specifically Deuteronomy, where it was customary to place a clean cloth on the bridal bed where the bride and groom would consummate their marriage, where the bride, if she was virgin, would release blood, and this blood on this cloth became evidence to the groom, the parents, and the city elders that the bride was a virgin.[3]

This was considered a blood covenant between a husband and a wife, and it was not some strange cultural deed that occurred in those days, but it was honored by God. Just as the innocent blood of animals was brought before the Lord as a sin offering so that the individual could be cleansed, the same is true during the first bridal night when two innocent individuals (virgins) come together in sexual intimacy and the blood is released from the woman, which becomes the blood convent between a man and a woman, which the Almighty God honors and considers holy and sacred.

But what happens when this blood covenant is not contained within the boundaries of a marriage covenant? Or what happens when two virgins have sexual relations but are not legally married? The divine covenant is then distorted and nullified. As the first bridal night is holy and sacred, this is now washed away because the virgin couple has also entered into a blood covenant, as the virgin girl releases blood during their sexual intercourse, but this release of blood was outside of the originally intended blood covenant that God has ordained.

Is this to say that those who have messed up in this area have no hope for the future? Certainly not! Can these same people get married and have a great marriage if they surrender their lives and marriage to God? Yes! But, having said that, there is something special and unique about two virgins marrying, as opposed to those who are not. And I've talked about this in detail in the previous chapter about soul ties and how your past memories will follow you for the rest of your life.

With that said, some may find this biased, implying that those who married as virgins are more special before God, which is not true, but because they chose to preserve their virginity, a special heavenly blessing was opened up into their marriage. For example, if a brand-new car is involved in a serious accident, it can always be repaired so well that an average person would never know. Now, someone can try to rig the system by reselling this car as if it were brand new, but if this lie is discovered, the seller will be in big trouble. Typically, this same new car is classified as salvaged, which significantly reduces its value. This same vehicle will never run as well as it did when it was brand new, and this same car will have issues much faster and more frequently because it has already been wrecked.

This same principle applies to our virginity, where those who are virgins are like brand new cars, and those who are not and made mistakes before they married can always be fully fixed by God and the power of Jesus' blood, but your virginity can never be one percent restored, just as the car cannot be restored to its original state. Hopefully, this has clarified this vital issue. Thank God once more for His mercy, grace, and forgiveness.

"WITH THE HELP OF THE ALMIGHTY GOD, YOUR SEXUAL PURITY HAS BEEN FULLY ENTRUSTED INTO YOUR HANDS FOR YOU TO PRESERVE AND PROTECT."

IS THERE STILL HOPE FOR SOMEONE LIKE ME?

It is very common for many people to feel condemned and hopeless simply because they are no longer virgins or have lived a sexually promiscuous lifestyle. This is not the case! And the Bible is full of passages that can give anyone a lot of hope because of the power of Jesus' blood, which is able to wash away any sin.

If you are reading this and are feeling either condemnation or conviction, I want to challenge you my friend to set this book aside and sincerely come before your heavenly Father and wholeheartedly bring your life or your past before Him and simply ask for His forgiveness, allowing the power of Jesus' blood to fully wash you and the power of the Holy Spirit to invade your heart and mind so you will have the full assurance that you are forgiven and that your sins are forgiven. And make this day the start of a brand-new chapter in your life so that you can live a life with significance.

"DO NOT LET YOUR PAST MISTAKES DERAIL YOU FROM LIVING OUT YOUR TRUE KINGDOM PURPOSE."

RATED "R" RECOMMENDATIONS

- Understand and value the significance of sexual purity.
- Find new friends if your current friends are influencing you in ungodly ways.

- If you're dating or in a relationship with someone and they're hinting at having sexual relations with you, drop that person like it's a bad habit.
- Don't be embarrassed because you're still a virgin. Wear it as a personal testimony in front of others.
- If you have made careless sexual choices, then seek God's forgiveness.
- Being a virgin before marriage may put you in an awkward position in front of some of your peers, but don't let that discourage you because the Lord will use you as a powerful tool of testimony in front of others.

9

DATING IS NOT ABOUT DO'S AND DON'TS

No one likes rules, regulations, or restrictions, or being controlled, especially if they are teenagers. This is all normal human behavior, as we all have free will, which our heavenly Father implanted in our human DNA. This principle also applies to dating, where dating isn't about do's and don'ts. And in this chapter, I'd like to lay out some fundamental principles that will help you see dating in a new light, or at the very least approach dating in an unconventional and non-legalistic manner.

COVENANT IN DATING (RELATIONSHIPS)

When I was engaged to my lovely bride at the time, we agreed on a few ground rules in the form of boundaries that we would not cross. One of them was that we would not kiss during our relationship and engagement period. And we stuck to our decision to have our first kiss on our wedding day. Now, without being labeled as a righteous zealot, we all have the right to make whatever decision we feel is right for us, and just because you kissed during your relationship season or while you were engaged does not make you a sinner or less of a Christian than me. The decision that I made with my bride was one that we both felt strongly about.

What does it mean to have a covenant in your dating or relationship? First and foremost, every person must have a serious relationship with the Lord and enter into a covenant with Him. Only then is it safe and recommended for anyone to enter into a relationship with someone else, because your current relationship will be derived from your personal covenant with the Lord, not from fleshy lustful appetites for the opposite sex.

Furthermore, having a specific dating covenant requires both individuals to follow some basic ground rules, or have strong boundaries, or be both in agreement with what you two will allow and what will be frowned upon. And Apostle Paul offers some insight into why it is important to have specific boundaries or restrictions while dating, saying: "Now concerning the things of which you wrote to me: *It is* good for a man not to touch a woman."[1] This single verse merely highlights the dangers of flirting with the opposite sex.

Again, dating may appear to be a wonderful thing because so many people do it, but what you allow will only worsen over time. Holding hands will become tedious at some point. Hugging will become boring. Kissing, on the other hand, will only arouse both of you to take it to the next level, as kissing is one of the most stimulating acts, and sex is the next most stimulating act.

Here are some healthy dating suggestions for those who choose to enter the dating season:

- *God has specifically designed all sexual and intimate relationships to take place within the confines of a marital covenant.*
- *God will only reveal His true nature to us if we make a covenant with Him.*
- *Set healthy boundaries for what is and is not permissible.*
- *If what you're doing is making you uncomfortable, that's a good sign that you should stop.*
- *If your relationship is distracting you from your relationship with the Lord, you should rethink your relationship.*
- *Never inappropriately touch each other, especially the most intimate body parts.*
- *As soon as your boyfriend/girlfriend asks or encourages you to have sex with them, the relationship should end immediately.*
- *Make an effort to never be alone at home or completely isolated in an area where there are no other people.*

This powerful statement was made by my dear friend Vitaly B., with whom I've been friends for many years, when we once tag-teamed to do a Rated R series for the youth in our local church, which focused on dating, relationships, marriage, and sexual purity. "You will never know the true person you are dating until you are in a covenant with them," he said. That was a powerful statement! And he expanded on this thought by saying, "God kept it a secret for a reason." And this is so true that no one will truly know the heart, nature, character, and hidden person while dating; only once they enter into a marriage covenant will they begin to unwrap each other like a layered onion.

"SETTING BOUNDARIES OR RESTRICTIONS IN DATING IS NOT INTENDED TO BIND YOU, BUT RATHER TO HOLD YOU ACCOUNTABLE BEFORE YOUR HEAVENLY FATHER."

DATING VS COURTING

Is there a distinction to be made between dating and courting? Both yes and no! In a nutshell, dating occurs when two people become interested in each other and take further action steps such as going on dates, spending time together, and developing a romantic relationship. This romantic relationship will differ from one person to the next. While courting is when two people have a strong interest in each other because they have already known each other through school, church, or the neighborhood and want to take the next step and become more serious about their relationship.

Both dating and courting have similar patterns and a few minor differences, but they are not dissimilar. So, whether you want to call your relationship with the opposite sex dating or courting, the main point is that you are still in a personal relationship with feelings, emotions, affection, and a certain level of sexual desire. And how far these feelings, affections, or sexual desires go is entirely up to you, as well as your ability to maintain self-control, the type of boundaries you establish in your relationship, and whether you abide in the fear of the Lord.

Again, you don't have to be too religious or spiritual to say you're courting someone, and you shouldn't be too naive to think that dating isn't a big deal because you're just trying to get to know the other person, because on the contrary, even in dating, you can become very attached to the other person, and this attachment can be sexual in nature. And, once again, my honest advice to all of you single people out there is to only engage in dating or courting if you are serious about taking your relationship to the next level, which is marriage.

"ANYONE WHO WISHES TO ENTER INTO A SERIOUS RELATIONSHIP MUST ALWAYS HAVE GOD AT THE CENTER, AND THE FEAR OF THE LORD AS THE PRIMARY DIRECTIVE."

RATED "R" RECOMMENDATIONS

- It is critical that when you date, you both intentionally set specific boundaries or rules to hold each other accountable.

- Make every effort not to isolate yourself from other people or potential witnesses while dating or courting. This is going to be one of your safeguards.
- Only after you have established a solid and stable relationship with the Lord should you consider dating or beginning a serious relationship.
- If your motivation for dating or courting is solely to have a boyfriend/girlfriend, you will expose yourself to temptations that will be difficult to resist.
- Any type of relationship must be approached with the fear of the Lord, as this will be one of the most powerful safeguards for both of you.

10

THE POWER OF CHOICES

There are numerous choices in life. Life is full of daily decisions, and the more serious your choices become as you get older. And, as our choices vary, some of them carry a lot of weight, and some of them may even have dire consequences. And once again, God's Word comes to our aid with this life-changing advice: "Don't team up with those who are unbelievers. How can righteousness be a partner with wickedness? How can light live with darkness? What harmony can there be between Christ and the devil? How can a believer be a partner with an unbeliever?"[1]

The preceding passage implies that we must make wise decisions about who we partner with, befriend, or even date. And in this chapter, I will draw a stark contrast between King David and Joseph, as well as discuss the law of sowing and reaping, the power of our choices, and the significance of fearing the Lord.

THE DIFFERENCE BETWEEN KING DAVID AND JOSEPH

The Bible is full of great biblical heroes and role models, two of whom are King David and Joseph. Both of them have accomplished much greatness and can teach us all valuable life lessons. One of these life lessons is about sexual integrity. At one point, King David and Joseph were exposed to a sexual environment, with David lustfully observing Bathsheba while she bathed, and Joseph being forcefully begged by Potiphar's wife to sleep with her, but Joseph ran away.

Both individuals were confronted with sexual temptations, but one succumbed while the other fled. There are several powerful takeaway lessons here. And the law of sowing and reaping will be covered in these lessons. Let us look at some of the differences between King David and Joseph in greater detail:

- **King David** – *Instead of walking away from his rooftop, he began to lust after Bathsheba.*
- **Joseph** – *Ran away from Potiphar's wife, who tried to sexually seduce him.*
- **King David** – *Because of his sexual appetites, David forced Bathsheba to have sex with him, despite the fact that she was married.*
- **Joseph** – *Because he was aware of his purpose and calling from God, he acted in fear of the Lord and fled.*
- **King David** – *When he discovered that Bathsheba had become pregnant as a result of his affair, he attempted to cover up his sinful deed by forcing Bathsheba's husband to sleep with his wife, which he refused.*

- **Joseph** – *Ran away naked from Potiphar's wife as she grabbed hold of his garments, which she used as evidence against Joseph, alleging that he attempted to rape her.*
- **King David** – *Because he was afraid of being caught, he put Bathsheba's husband in the front lines of the battle, which resulted in his death.*
- **Joseph** – *Was eventually charged with a crime and imprisoned for the rest of his life.*
- **King David** – *Takes Bathsheba as another wife, but their child of fornication dies as a result of God's judgment.*
- **Joseph** – *Despite being falsely accused, he continued to function in his kingdom abilities, and the chief guard appointed him as a person of authority in the prison cell.*
- **King David** – *After one of his sons (Amnon) sexually raped his daughter (Tamar), Absalom murders Amnon in revenge.*
- **Joseph** – *While in prison he interpreted dreams for the baker and the butler, who were Pharaohs inner circle.*
- **King David** – *Later on, Absalom plots a coup against his father, forcing David to flee his kingdom.*
- **Joseph** – *After being imprisoned for many years, he was brought before Pharaoh to interpret his dreams.*
- **King David** – *On the palace rooftop, his son Absalom has forcible sex with David's concubines.*
- **Joseph** – *Gets promoted from the pit into the palace.*
- **King David** – *Becomes an outcast and is forced to flee and hide from his son Absalom.*
- **Joseph** – *Eventually, he becomes Pharaoh's right hand, with complete authority over Egypt.*
- **King David** – *After his son Absalom is killed, he returns to his broken-down kingdom.*

- **Joseph** – *Pharaoh's daughter is married to him, and he saves the Egyptian kingdom from famine.*

The preceding outline is heart wrenching and dramatically demonstrates the difference between what happened in David's life and what happened in Joseph's life, which was all due to the choices they made in relation to their sexual temptation. Is the above comparison implying that Joseph is super holy, and King David is an evil adulterer? No! Is Joseph more beloved by God than David? No! Or perhaps God showed favoritism towards Joseph? No, once more! The principle to remember here is the law of sowing and reaping. David was unable to control his lustful appetites, whereas Joseph was.

As much as all of the preceding shows almost opposite outcomes, it does highlight the notion of the powerful side effects of sexual sins, which can sweep your life away like a tidal wave. But I also want to emphasize another important point here: no matter how treacherous and horrific King David's deeds were, God still referred to him as "a man after His own heart."[2] This is a profound truth, but it begs the question, "Why?" It's because David understood God's heart, as well as the significance of repentance.

The power of consequences of your choices and the power of redemption can be summed up in the story of David and Joseph. As a result, our heavenly Father is both good and wonderful. And I suppose a question could be asked: Did my previous choices place me in the path of King David or Joseph? Whatever the case may be, know that there is still a future and hope for you, my friend.

"YOUR CHOICES TODAY, WHETHER GOOD OR BAD, WILL BECOME LIKE SEEDS THAT WILL BEAR FRUIT IN THE FUTURE."

THE KINGDOM LAW OF SOWING AND REAPING

We've all heard pastors, preachers, and parents say it a million times: "What you sow is what you will reap."[3] This is a kingdom law that operates flawlessly throughout the world, and even if an individual chooses to ignore, eradicate, or cast off this law, it is still a law in God's eyes. And because our choices are subject to this universal law, our wrong choices will produce a negative harvest, whereas our right or good choices will produce a healthy harvest that will bring us much pleasure and satisfaction.

God instituted the kingdom law of sowing and reaping not as harsh rules and regulations to make us uncomfortable, but as spiritual guardrails to keep us from going over the edge and bringing much destruction into our personal lives. Furthermore, the law of sowing and reaping contains many kingdom blessings that our heavenly Father desires to release into our lives, families, marriages, and business ventures.

As we freely give ourselves the liberty to make whatever choices and decisions we want, the kingdom law of sowing and reaping will always be by our side, reminding us of the potential blessings or punishments that could result from that particular choice. And the decisions we make in dating, relationships, and marriage will bear specific fruits, as our choices become a type of seed that we sow into our personal lives.

THE POWER OF CHOICES

The choices we make on a daily basis have enormous power. The decisions you make today will shape your future, and sometimes these decisions come with a hefty price tag that you will have to bear for the rest of your life. And the Bible is not shy about discussing our daily choices, and it is also full of passages that specifically address the topics of adultery, fornication, and sexual immorality. Let's take a look at how many different references the Bible has to say about this important topic:

- Adultery – 36 times in the Bible
- Fornication – 14 times
- Lust – 42 times
- Sexual Immorality – 18 times

Why do I make choices appear to be powerful? Because our decisions have a lot of clout. These choices will either powerfully usher in blessings or painful regrets. And God has created us in such a way that we must make choices in our daily lives, as choices shape our inner character and mindset, choices allow us to mature, and most importantly, choices allow us to be wrong and make mistakes. Yes, being wrong and making mistakes is a normal and healthy part of the learning process, but making foolish, arrogant, and ungodly decisions is not, because these types of decisions are made out of a lack of knowledge, but a lack of fear of the Lord.

"YOUR CHOICES TODAY WILL EVENTUALLY SHAPE YOUR FUTURE."

WALK DAILY IN THE FEAR OF THE LORD

The wise King Solomon defined the fear of the Lord in some of the most profound ways, and those who choose to abide in the fear of the Lord will unlock heavenly blessings. You see, fear of the Lord will serve as a navigation system for your life, spiritual growth, marriage, and kingdom purpose. Furthermore, the fear of the Lord will act as a lifejacket in your life, keeping you from drowning in the lustful appetites of the world.

Those who choose to abide in the fear of the Lord place themselves under divine protection, because the fear of the Lord acts in your life like a fire extinguisher, protecting you from the fires of hell. Furthermore, fear of the Lord acts as an X-ray, allowing you to see what is going on in your heart. This also serves as a daily spiritual checkup, which is essential for your spiritual growth.

The fear of the Lord is like superglue that keeps you connected to God's will for your life at all times. And the fear of the Lord will become like rocket fuel, propelling your faith to new heights. And this same fear of the Lord will assist you in making the right decisions about whom you should date, how far you should take your relationship with another person or making the critical decision of either proposing to her or saying "yes" to the one you love. All of the above will become a reality if you choose to live your life in fear of the Lord.

"THE FEAR OF THE LORD WILL SERVE AS A DAILY BODYGUARD, PROTECTING YOU AGAINST SIN, PRIDE, SELFISHNESS, AND THE PATH OF DESTRUCTION."

RATED "R" RECOMMENDATIONS

- Because our choices have great power, consider the outcome of King David's choices in comparison to Joseph's.
- The fear of the Lord will be like a box of crayons, adding color to your life.
- Choose to live with the same heart attitude as Joseph did.
- When you abide in the fear of the Lord, it will then serve you as your daily bodyguard, protecting you against sin, wrong people, immoral behaviors, or sexual temptations.
- Making the right choices will strengthen your spiritual foundation, while making the wrong choices will cause many cracks in it.

11

KNOW YOUR TIME AND SEASONS

A day has a twenty-four-hour cycle that the entire world operates and functions according to. It is normal for many people to wake up in the morning to go about their daily lives, and it is also normal for most people to sleep at night. It is also common sense for any farmer to sow the seeds in the spring in order to harvest the ripe harvest in the fall season, whereas almost no farmer sows in the winter. This is also true when it comes to knowing our time and seasons in life.

There is a season when we must attend school. Then there comes a time and season for us to graduate from school and pursue a full-time job, a corporate career, or start our own business. There is also a proper time for someone to become pregnant or marry. But how would it appear if a ten-year-old had to get up early to go to work instead of school? Or a fifteen-year-old girl becoming pregnant? Or two middle schoolers who want to marry right away because they love each other? All of the preceding will make you cringe, as common-sense dictates that it is not the appropriate time to do all of the preceding. And the author of Ecclesiastes sheds some light on this idea when he says, "To everything *there is* a season, A time for every purpose under heaven."[1]

Knowing your time and seasons is critical because they will assist you in properly prioritizing your life. In light of the preceding scripture, here are some suggestions for understanding time and seasons:

- There is a time and season *to fall in love.*
- There is a time and season *to start a serious relationship.*
- There is a time and season *to say, "No!"*
- There is a time and season *to be single and to get married.*
- There is a time and season *to build a strong personal relationship with Jesus.*
- There is a time and season *to stay focused on the current priorities in your life (education, career, growing your business).*
- There is a time and season *to safe up enough money for your future.*

Furthermore, Solomon in one of his love songs had a wise recommendation, "Oh, let me warn you, sisters in Jerusalem: Don't excite love, don't stir it up, until the time is ripe – and you're ready."[2] And in this chapter, I'd like to clarify the meaning of the phrase "I'm in love," as well as the significance of having your priorities straight.

I'M IN LOVE

Being in love, falling in love, having someone love you, or having an interest in someone may all sound similar, but they each mean something different. True love is a divine experience that our heavenly Father has programmed into every living human being. And true love can only come from above, as everything else is a feeling that is frequently triggered by one's own fleshly desires.

Teenagers frequently utter childish phrases like, "He loves me!" "She's madly in love with me!" "We absolutely love each other!" This sounds cute, especially coming from the lips of a fifteen-year-old with acne on their face. The phrase or statement "I'm in love" should not be used carelessly, as these words are powerful and have a divine meaning.

If you are not ready for a serious relationship that will eventually lead you to the wedding alter, then every time someone, such as your boyfriend or girlfriend, says these words, simply brush them aside, as they honestly do not carry any weight or true meaning. Yes, this may be a harsh statement on my part, but we now live in a society where words or phrases that used to have powerful meanings have been simply degraded, simply because we do not understand the true meaning of certain words or phrases. And this has also become a form of deception and manipulation, as we freely express ourselves while our hearts are far from what we just said.

I wholeheartedly believe that true love comes from above, as our heavenly Father downloads into our hearts and allows that true love to come forth when we are ready and mature enough to move into the next season of our relationship. This happened to me; I had been friends with my bride for over a year before we began a serious relationship, and it wasn't until then that I told her I loved her. So, falling in love is an exhilarating experience that is nearly impossible to describe. However, you must fully entrust this aspect of your life to your heavenly Father, who knows your time and seasons without a doubt.

"LOVE IS A POWERFUL FORCE THAT CAN EITHER LIFT YOU UP OR CAUSE YOU A LOT OF PAIN AND HEARTACHE."

HAVING YOUR PRIORITIES STRAIGHT

When God created Adam, the first thing He told him to do was "work."[3] The second truth we discover is that God, the Creator, spent quality time with Adam, teaching him many things, including not to eat from the tree of the knowledge of good and evil and allowing Adam to release his abilities when God presented animals before him to see what Adam would call them. And, from a theological standpoint, no one can say for certain how long Adam and Eve lived in the Garden of Eden. Or, more specifically, how long was Adam alone without Eve by his side?

And it was only while Adam was working and maintaining the Garden, as well as abiding in God's presence, that God said: Then the Lord God said, "It is not good for the man to be alone. I will make a helper who is just right for him."[4] This outlines God's divine wisdom and order once more, which should become the foundational truth for anyone desiring to marry that the first thing you need to do is be busy and occupied with the gifts, skills, talent, and kingdom potential that your heavenly Father has equipped you with. And by staying focused on your kingdom assignment, you will avoid being easily distracted by the opposite sex or becoming bored, both of which can lead to making poor decisions in life. And the second thing is that being in God's presence and seeking His face on a regular basis helps you grow stronger in your relationship with Him. And as you grow in your faith, the Holy Spirit will give you wisdom and sound advice for making the right decisions in your life, as well as protect your heart from becoming attached or attracted to someone if it is not your season to enter into a serious relationship.

And if you make these two things your top priorities, King Solomon's wise words will ring true in your life: "A man's heart plans his way, but the Lord directs his steps."[5] And one more powerful advice: "There are many plans in a man's heart, nevertheless the Lord's counsel – that will stand."[6]

When you and I align our priorities in accordance with God's purpose and will, He will properly and in His time direct our steps, clear the path in front of us, and begin to open doors that need to be opened as well as close doors that need to be closed in this season of our lives. And Jesus wisely added: "But seek first the kingdom of God and His righteousness, and all these things shall be added to you."[7] The key words here are "all these things," which means your heavenly Father has already provided for all of your needs, including your future spouse.

My friend, I challenge you to prioritize your life in accordance with His perfect will for your life, and don't worry about when you'll find the love of your life or when you'll get married; with the help of the Holy Spirit, you'll be able to know and discern your time and seasons.

> *"PRIORITIES ARE LIKE IKEA'S STEP-BY-STEP INSTRUCTION MANUAL, SHOWING YOU EXACTLY WHAT ORDER YOU NEED TO FOLLOW TO COMPLETE YOUR CURRENT ASSIGNMENT."*

RATED "R" RECOMMENDATIONS

- It is essential to know your time and seasons of life. Each season of your life has a distinct purpose and an assignment that you must complete.
- The word "love" and its meaning are extremely powerful. It should not be used lightly.
- If you do not set the right priorities in your life, then someone else will.
- Time will never be your best friend, but it can be a useful guide.
- Seasons come and go, so don't be afraid of the one you're in right now.

12

THE POWER OF A MARRIAGE COVENANT

Marriage is one of the oldest, if not the oldest, institution that has existed since the dawn of time. And the Bible is replete with passages, illustrations, and examples relating to what marriage is, the purpose of marriage, the significance of marriage, and the sanctity of a marriage covenant. And in this powerful chapter, I want to emphasize the significance of marriage as a covenant and marriage as divinely sacred.

WHAT IS A MARRIAGE COVENANT?

We've all heard that marriage is a covenant, not a contract, so why are there so many divorces in the body of Christ? If the covenant is meant to be for the rest of one's life, why do more than 60% of Christian marriages fail? Furthermore, could we say that whenever a couple shares their marriage vows on their wedding day, those vows are just traditional words that everyone says, with no substance? Certainly not!

Marriage is a covenant that began in the Garden of Eden with the Almighty Creator's statement: "Then the Lord God said, 'It is not good for the man to be alone. I will make a helper who is just right for him.'"[1] Our heavenly Father knew from the beginning of time that it is not good for men and women to live alone, because living together makes life much more adventurous and fulfilling, and it also allows mankind to procreate and multiply on this earth.

Furthermore, marriage allows two separate people to channel their creativity, potential, and abilities into their marriage covenant and form a unique family that solely depends on each other as they are able to complete one another throughout their lives. And marriage is a covenant because it requires two separate individuals to invest everything they have in order for this covenant to last until their dying breath.

And God, our Creator, perfectly knew from the beginning that marriage would not be easy, and would be full of hardships, because marriage, in a nutshell, is an institution of two selfish individuals who frequently become overly concerned with their own well-being, rather than the well-being of their spouse, and marriage provides the opportunity for these two selfish individuals to learn how to serve one another with the same heart attitude as our heavenly Father.

"MARRIAGE IS A LIFELONG ADVENTURE, NOT A SEASONAL EVENT."

MARRIAGE IS SACRED

Why is marriage sacred? Because God the Father has made it sacred! Marriage is a distinctive covenant union between a man and a woman in which God can demonstrate and reveal His divine purpose to His children. And, because marriage is sacred, Jesus shared some sobering words about His stance on divorce: "Furthermore it has been said, 'Whoever divorces his wife, let him give her a certificate of divorce,' but I say to you that whoever divorces his wife for any reason except sexual immorality causes her to commit adultery; and whoever marries a woman who is divorced commits adultery."[2]

Except for sexual immorality, the above passage is strict and straightforward, and it demonstrates that Jesus and God the Father are not in favor of divorce. This reinforces the notion that marriage is sacred once more. Period! And there are some Christians who are looking for loopholes to undo the "I do," and the majority of divorces among Christians are not related to sexual immorality.

Moreover, the sacredness of marriage serves a greater purpose in God's eyes, as the union of two individuals is powerful, with two being able to accomplish far more together than those who choose to remain single. When a husband and wife are united in their hearts, spirits, and kingdom purpose, this couple becomes powerful and influential. And this is one of the primary reasons why the devil works tirelessly to create a schism or a barrier between couples, not allowing them to fully function as a power unit. And, so far, the enemy of our souls has done an excellent job, but I believe we are truly living in such opportune times where our heavenly Father is raising power couples with strong marriages who will be able to do amazing things on earth. However, if you want to be this power couple, you must understand that marriage is sacred.

"MARRIAGE IS A SACRED INSTITUTION." PERIOD! AND NO MATTER HOW HARD SOMEONE TRIES TO CHANGE OR REDEFINE MARRIAGE, IT WILL ALWAYS BE WHAT GOD INTENDED IT TO BE."

RATED "R" RECOMMENDATIONS

- Whether you are single or married, please grab a hold of the revelation that there is power in a marriage covenant.
- Marriage is sacred. Period!
- Marriage was created in heaven, but the pits of hell are working nonstop to destroy this marriage covenant.
- Marriage should never be viewed as something that places shackles on two individuals, but rather as something powerful and full of blessings.
- While you are single, abide in a strong covenant with your Creator, and when you do get married, likewise abide in that marriage covenant.

13

IT IS NOT GOOD TO BE ALONE

When we read the Bible, we have the option of accepting the Word as the truth, simple recommendations, or just plain suggestions or good thoughts from historical figures. However, God's words are His words, not man's, and God did have some wise words to say to those who are single: Then the Lord God said, "It is not good for the man to be alone. I will make a helper who is just right for him."[1]

God's recommendation above was that "it is not good." God did not say that being single is bad, horrible, or unbiblical, but rather that "it is not good." So, you can choose to live alone without ever marrying and fully devote your life, your free time, and your potential to God, and you will be fine. One of my aunts has chosen a life of celibacy and is doing well; she has completely dedicated her life to serving the Lord.

Having said that, loneliness and feeling alone have and continue to drive people to drink, engage in substance abuse, suffer from depression, and even commit suicide. This is also true in terms of marriage. We now live in an upside-down society in which marriage is no longer a high priority, and many people marry later in life. And in this chapter, I wanted to emphasize the importance of marriage, why marriage is not as old-fashioned as some believe, and why your future wife will become your helper, and your future husband will be your provider, protector, and priest. You will also learn about the myth of finding the right person and the power of being in a relationship.

MARRIAGE IS OLD SCHOOL

It is unsurprising that this generation has not only redefined marriage but has also labeled it as "old school" or "not a vital part of someone's life." If God did not value marriage, he would not say, "It is not good for the man (or woman) to be alone."[2] Marriage is not an old-fashioned institution, and what has changed in our current culture is that some people do not want to commit to a long-term marriage covenant, while others enjoy living a life of freedom in which they can date whomever they want and engage in sexual relationships with whomever their lustful heart desires. Furthermore, our culture has been redefining marriage, family, and how to raise children, and many people have a distorted view of marriage.

However, the Bible paints a very different picture of marriage for us. Marriage removes loneliness, marriage gives the individual a reason to constantly love and care for the other, and marriage also has the privilege of bringing forth new life into this world, where both parents will enjoy their family life on a whole new level.

"WHAT GOD HAS CREATED AND ESTABLISHED CAN NEVER BE NULLIFIED OR ELIMINATED BY MAN."

YOUR WIFE WILL BE YOUR HELPER

If you are a guy who is thinking about getting married, here are some of the benefits that come with being married. As I have previously stated, God desired to create a "helper" for Adam, and this is one of the best definitions for any wife, that she will become a helper to her husband. A helper does not imply that she will do everything for him, but rather that she will assist him in carrying out his kingdom purpose and assignment on earth.

In the Message translation of the Bible, I like the use of the word "companion," instead of helper and the Thesaurus expounds on the meaning of companion as: assistant, co-worker, guide, and partner. That is extremely powerful. So, in a nutshell, your future wife will work with you to build a family and raise children in order to fulfill God's will. She will also serve as your assistant and coworker as you both work to build God's kingdom on Earth.

YOUR HUSBAND WILL BE YOUR PROTECTOR, PROVIDER AND PRIEST

If you are a girl who is seriously considering marriage, here are some of the benefits you will receive as a result of your marriage. God has appointed your future husband to be your provider, protector, and priest. And, as a married man, Apostle Peter shared a powerful insight, saying: "In the same way, you husbands must give honor to your wives. Treat your wife with understanding as you live together. She may be weaker than you are, but she is your equal partner in God's gift of new life."[3]

The above passage's powerful key takeaways are that the wife may be weaker, but she is an "equal partner," and the husband "must give honor," which means giving her the much-needed attention, praise, and recognition. And, having been married for twenty years, I can attest to the accuracy of the above. This Bible passage emphasizes the husband as the protector.

In addition, the husband is regarded as the provider. And Timothy adds to this biblical principle when he says: "But if anyone does not provide for his own, especially for those of his household, he has denied the faith and is worse than an unbeliever."[4] This is a bold statement from Timothy, that if the husband is lazy or neglects his family's well-being, he has "denied the faith" that is so important to his walk with the Lord, and he is now "worse than an unbeliever." That should send shivers down every husband's spiritual spine.

Again, being a provider does not simply imply that you have a stable job and that your family can eat, have a roof over their heads, and clothes on their backs, but it also implies that you, as a husband, must do everything and anything to ensure that your family is well taken care of, even if it means getting a second job or working overtime every week.

Finally, the husband is your priest, who is solely responsible for the spiritual health of the marriage as well as the spiritual health of the entire family. Yes, it is no secret that many so-called Christian husbands have abandoned their responsibilities as priests in favor of working more and justifying themselves as primary providers and even protectors. That may appear to be fine for a short time, but when finances fail, health declines, and other various trials and issues of life arise, this is where the priest is needed, but if that priest is not present, the marriage will be jeopardized. And, as I previously stated, one of the primary reasons why many marriages fail is that the husband and wife do not have a stable relationship with Jesus, or where the husband has completely neglected his role and responsibility as a priest.

Again, God gave Adam the commandment not to eat of the tree of knowledge of good and evil in the beginning, so when Adam and Eve committed a sinful act of disobedience, God was not looking for Eve, and God was not inquiring from Eve, but God was looking for Adam and rebuking him. The same principle applies in marriage: the husband is the primary responsibility for the spiritual environment in any marriage, and the wife is only his helper in this sphere.

"YOUR HEAVENLY FATHER KNOWS THE RIGHT PEOPLE TO SURROUND YOU WITH IN ORDER FOR YOU TO FULFILL OUR KINGDOM PURPOSE."

THE MYTH OF FINDING THE RIGHT ONE

There are numerous myths about dating, relationships, and marriage that have developed over time. One of the myths addresses a critical question that many people have: "Is there only one right person for me to marry?" As important as this question is, it would be far too easy to give a religious answer by simply saying, "yes."

Let us return to the beginning of time. When God created Adam, He observed what Adam was doing after a while and said, "*It is* not good that man should be alone."[5] And the Almighty God made a helper for Adam, and when Adam awoke from his slumber, there she was, Eve. And this model can easily be taken out of context by interpreting it to mean that God only designed that one specific soulmate, just as Adam only had Eve and no other options. This belief, or even theology, could be very misleading, as we can closely observe current marriages among Christian people, including those in your local church, and find tens of thousands of couples who remarried after a divorce or after their first spouses died.

And the toe-curling question is, who is the true spouse? Or how will these particular spouses reunite in heaven when the wife was the first to die and her husband remarried? As I don't want to get too technical here, the belief or understanding that God has only set aside one specific person for you to marry may mislead and bind many people. After their wives died, I know pastors who remarried in their 50s and 60s. I also know people who were engaged but then called off the wedding and remarried under a different name and are now happily married. And I know people who divorced after a few years of marriage, even with children, after discovering that their spouse withheld vital information about their medical conditions, putting the marriage in jeopardy and causing much trauma. And, once again, these people remarried and are happy.

Again, the belief that there is only one right person for you is a myth, and we as God's children should not bind ourselves with legalism and unbiblical thinking. And, if this is the case, how should one approach the marriage institution as a whole? One thing that does give us a lot of insight is that God's Word is divine and universal, and the truths written in the Bible will work for those who want to submit to them. For example, if an unbelieving couple lives in accordance with the Word of God by remaining faithful to one another, being honest, loving and supporting one another, the Word of God will usher in blessings into their marriage even if they are not saved and do not believe in Jesus. How is this possible? Again, the living Word of God cannot be limited to Christian churchgoers. Because it is God's word, not man's limited ideologies.

This is also true in financial matters. Many wealthy people do not read the Bible or understand the concept of tithes and offerings, but they have a very giving heart, which is one of the main reasons they are so financially successful. On the other hand, there are many Christian folks who read the Bible and are well aware of tithes and offerings, but they are stingy and covetous, which is why they remain poor and live paycheck to paycheck.

Again, as we turn to the Word of God for clarification, Apostle Paul writes: "A wife is bound by law as long as her husband live; but if her husband dies, she is at liberty to be married to whom she wishes, only in the Lord."[6] Two vital points are that she has the freedom to marry whomever she wants as long as the new husband is a believer in the Lord, which is one of the most important points here. This passage alleviates the burden of trying to find the right one, or the one and only, that God has chosen from among the more than seven billion people on this planet.

Another intriguing insight is the belief that many people are looking for the best compatible individual who would make the best fit for their life, interests, and heart's desire. But when we go to the root meaning of the word *compatible*, in Latin it's called "compati," and the meaning of *compati* is: to suffer with. Hopefully this will clear up any type of delusional belief that many may have about searching for the most compatible mate.[7]

"WHEN IT COMES TO MARRIAGE, DON'T GET CAUGHT UP IN MAN-MADE MYTHS OR IDEOLOGIES."

THE POWER OF TWO

There is strength in unity. When two people agree, they have power. And there is greater success when individuals work as one team to complete a specific task. This same divine principle applies to marriage when a husband and wife walk and live in complete unity in accordance with God's perfect will for their life and marriage. And Ecclesiastes contains a powerful passage that describes the power of two: "Two are better than one, because they have a good reward for their labor. For if they fall, one will lift up his companion. But woe to him who is alone when he falls, for he has no one to help him up. Again, if two lie down together, they will keep warm; but how can one be warm alone? Though one may be overpowered by another, two can withstand him. And threefold cord is not quickly broken."[8]

Similarly, whenever a couple decides to do something together, they automatically function as a power couple, able to accomplish more in a much shorter amount of time. This is true in the areas of finances, business growth, raising children, and serving in their kingdom assignment. And in my life, I've seen such seemingly unstable couples who did not function as two, but selfishly chose to do things on their own. And whenever we as God's children understand this divine law, we become a blessing to one another, a blessing to our local church, and even a blessing to our society.

And as I close this lengthy chapter, I want to encourage you, my fellow brother and sister in the Lord, that if you are single, know your time and seasons, but if you are of that mature age, boldly venture towards a marriage covenant because life with your spouse will be much more satisfying. But if you are married, I strongly advise you to become one in order to unleash the power of two and watch what the heavenly Father will do in your marriage and through both of you.

"THE POWER OF TWO WILL ALWAYS OUTPERFORM THOSE WHO CHOOSE TO GO IT ALONE."

RATED "R" RECOMMENDATIONS

- It is not good to be alone. Period!
- There is tremendous power when two individuals decide to do life together, especially in a marriage covenant.
- Do not bombard yourself with various myths that pertain to finding that right person.
- Your future wife will be the best gift that God has in store for you.
- Your future husband will be the greatest blessings that you will ever experience.
- For some marriage is old school, but for you marriage will become the greatest institute where you will obtain the diploma called, "life."

14

BEFORE YOU SAY "I DO"

It was December 1st, 2001, and the sky was blue, and the warm weather allowed me to wear a t-shirt, which is unusual for this time of year in New England Massachusetts. Why do I recall this event so vividly? This was the day I proposed to my lovely and sexy bride. And, as you may have guessed, she said "yes!" Since that time, I've been the luckiest and most blessed man on the planet.

To be completely honest and open with you, I was both excited and nervous. Was I worried that she'd say, "No!" Not exactly! I was nervous because what I was about to do meant that this person would be spending the rest of her life with me. And before I took the daring step of proposing to my bride, I did everything I could to ensure that this was the right time and season for me to embark on this new chapter of my life. And, like her, I was on fire for the Lord at that time in my life. And we were both involved in ministry and held steady jobs.

In this chapter, I will take you deep sea diving as you discover and learn the importance before you say "I do" and before you propose to the love of your life. Here, I will firmly address the significance of what you, as a guy, should be aware of, as well as what difficult questions you may need to ask the one you love. And as a girl, what you need to know about the person you might want to spend the rest of your life with. The questions outlined in this chapter are difficult, challenging, and extremely sobering because they are designed to capture your attention on a whole new level. And the reason I chose to address these critical questions is because I have seen many marriages fail.

THE TEN COMMANDMENTS BEFORE YOU SAY I DO

There is an abundance of literature available that contains advice, suggestions, and recommendations on what constitutes a perfect relationship, a dream wedding, or a lasting marriage. On the surface, that literature may appear credible on the cover page, but the majority of them are not basing all of their advice or recommendations on the Word of God; it is solely secular, and is frequently written by individuals who are divorced, have had numerous unsuccessful relationships, and a slew of other nonsense.

Before you say, "I do!" I wanted to give you some practical, personal, and biblical advice on what I call the ten commandments. And some of these suggestions may appear strange, practical, amusing, or far too profound. But, having had the opportunity to mentor youth for many years and seeing a sad pattern repeat itself in broken marriages, I wholeheartedly believe that these questions are critical. So, let's take a look at some of these commandments that pertain specifically to the girls:

For Girls:

1. ***Does he have a stable or a credible job?***
   - As much as this may seem obvious, love can be far too blind and naive at times.
2. ***What is his current relationship with the lord?***
   - If he has no relationship with the Lord, is not born-again, and does not regularly attend church, then red flags should be raised. This alone will be sufficient to declare, "I don't!"
   - Furthermore, this has been one of the leading causes of divorces and broken marriages among Christians, where she believed she could change him. This is one of the devil's most egregious lies.
3. ***Does he have credit card debt?***
   - One of the leading causes of divorce and broken marriages is financial insecurity, which is frequently the result of maxed-out credit cards and irresponsible money spending.
   - There is good debt and there is bad debt.
   - Any form of credit card debt is very unhealthy.
   - If he has excessive credit card debt, that must be addressed before you say, "I do!"
4. ***Is he the only child in the family?***
   - This is a unique question because it may appear to be completely irrelevant, but in my experience, I have seen a pattern where the wife was too demanding and selfish, or the husband was unable to effectively function as a leader because mama was constantly pampering him throughout his entire life, and continues to do so even after he married.

5. ***Is he a virgin?***
   - This was one of the first questions my late father-in-law asked me when I approached him to ask for his daughter's hand in marriage.
   - Furthermore, this question contains a number of truths and facts that may lead you, as the prospective bride, to make the bold decision to end your relationship.
   - Moreover, by asking this serious question, you will be able to learn if he is honest and transparent with you, which will play a significant role in your future marriage.
   - Also, if he is not a virgin, ask him to share about his previous life before knowing the Lord, so you can determine whether this was a one-time occurrence or a pattern of promiscuity. Again, this question is about soul ties, which I discussed in much detail in Chapter six.

6. ***What is his relationship with his parents (mom and dad)?***
   - This question will reveal his relationship with his father and mother.
   - If the parents are divorced or one of them lives in another state, then how often does he call or visit.
   - And if he is not living under the same roof, then how often does he visit them.

7. ***Does he have a child out of wedlock?***
   - This is an important question because men may have a child with a girl from another state or even another country. Years ago, a young Christian guy told me that he has a child living in another country that he has yet to tell his current wife about.

- And if he has a child out of wedlock, you must make a serious decision about whether you are willing to live with the fact that your potential future husband has fathered another child who is not your own.

8. ***Does he have any criminal history/record (imprisoned)?***
   - Depending on the nature of the crime, this will also shed light on his character and persona.
   - Furthermore, if he has a criminal record, how will it affect his ability to find a successful job or obtain a loan from a bank?

9. ***Does he have any medical issues or is he taking any serious prescriptions?***
   - Medical issues vary, and it is very common in our over-medicated society for a great amount of people to be on some kind of medication.
   - While medical issues vary, there are a few that should not be overlooked. Some of these medical issues, however, cannot be cured or even suppressed by medication because they are spiritual rather than physical in nature. According to the Bible, demons were responsible for certain disorders and medical symptoms that people experienced. Just a thought!
   - If he is taking serious prescription drugs that suppress his anger, rage, suicidal thoughts, or violent behavior, a loud alarm should sound off.
   - I'm aware of marriages that failed because one spouse chose not to disclose a serious medical issue, resulting in the spouse suffering and living in an abusive environment.

10. ***Does he have additive habits to video games or pornography?***

- Some may consider this question to be immature, but please read on to understand the deeper meaning behind this crucial question.
- In a recent study, it's been said that about 15% of divorces occurred because the husband was addicted to video games.[1]
- This problem is getting worse by the year, as men are unable to let go of their boyhood and become the Godly men that their wives and families require.
- I recently spoke with a young man in his late twenties who divorced due to a video game addiction.
- The WHO (World Health Organization) has officially recognized that gaming disorder is a mental condition.[2]
- I already discussed the destructive dangers of pornography in chapter three, and this should not be overlooked during your relationship.
- Porn is extremely addictive, and if it is not dealt with prior to marriage, it will infiltrate your future bedroom.
- Porn addiction binds a person to masturbation, which spills over into the marriage bedroom, where the guy gets more satisfaction from masturbation rather than his wife.
- Porn addiction will become a common occurrence in the bedroom as he seeks to be stimulated by watching someone having sex and then attempt to fulfill those same lustful desires through his wife.

- Porn has never helped a marriage. Never! This addiction must be confronted and dealt with if an engagement ring is to be received in the interim.

All of the above questions are not intended to bind you or make you appear odd, nor are they intended to create skepticism between the two of you. And these crucial questions should not be taken out of context. These questions could be a life-or-death situation, preventing you from experiencing major heartbreak, abuse, or divorce within seven-year period.

"ASKING QUESTIONS HAS ALWAYS BEEN ONE OF THE MOST FUNDAMENTAL RESPONSIBILITIES OF EVERY INDIVIDUAL, AS IT ALLOWS US TO GROW, DISCOVER, AND BROADEN OUR PERSPECTIVES ON LIFE."

THE TEN COMMANDMENTS BEFORE YOU PROPOSE

I've made some difficult decisions and plenty of stupid ones in my brief life. And one of the most difficult decisions I had to make was whether or not to propose to the love of my life. What made it so difficult? Because I knew that this was more than just asking someone to go on a one-time date with me; it was offering someone to accompany me on a lifelong journey until death separated us both. And with such a long-term commitment, you can bet it's not an easy decision to make.

And common sense will tell you that before making a serious decision, such as buying a house, starting a new job, or possibly moving to another state, you should carefully evaluate all of the necessary factors to ensure that this is the best decision for you and your family. And it's no different when it comes to proposing to your future wife. And as is customary, it is the guy who naturally proposes to a girl, so this places a slightly heavier burden on the guy's shoulders.

Let's take a stroll through some of the important questions that every guy should seriously consider asking the potential bride-to-be before proposing to her:

For Guys:

1. ***What is her relationship with her parents?***
   - As simple as this question may seem, it will tell you what kind of relationship she will have with you.
   - If she disrespects or dishonors her father as easily as her mother does, this will undoubtedly be a problem in marriage.
   - Furthermore, it is one of God's commandments for children to honor their parents.
   - Whether her parents are devout Christians or staunch atheists, she must respect and honor them.
2. ***Has she ever been raped or sexually molested?***
   - This is a heartfelt question to ponder during your relationship/engagement season.
   - Why is this such an important question? Because if she has ever been subjected to such a heinous and traumatic violation, it is critical that she has been fully healed and delivered from such abuse. If she hasn't, then this malicious abuse will accompany her into

marriage as a heavy and dark baggage. This frequently leads to her being closed to intimacy or rejecting you as her husband whenever you approach her intimately.

- This type of sexual trauma is so severe that it can take years for the girl/woman to fully recover emotionally, mentally, and spiritually.
- If this demonic act was committed by a family member, then has it been dealt with legally, or is it still a closely guarded secret that no one knows about? If there is a secret, it must be dealt with immediately.

3. Does she have any credit card debt?

- There is good debt and there is bad debt.
- If she has maxed out her credit cards, find out what the most frequently purchased items were.
- Learning where her spending habits go will give you an idea of whether or not her spending habits are unhealthy, which will also become the same spending habits in your marriage.

4. Is she the only child?

- Some may dismiss this question as meaningless because many families only have one child, but that is not the point I want to make here. Being the only child has its advantages in the short term, but it also has disadvantages in the long run.
- Despite the fact that no child has control over how many siblings they will have because that is entirely up to the parents, having only one child is often due to selfishness on the part of the parents and is only rarely due to medical or other reasons.

- Being the only child psychologically shapes them differently than having another sibling or a slew of siblings because it allows the child to interact, learn to play, fight and struggle together, and form other important social skills. Many of these life skills may be lacking in those who are the family's only child.
- Does this imply that she will not be a good wife? No! However, it is something to keep in mind.

5. *Is she a virgin?*
   - This question is just as important as the one a prospective bride-to-be asks her boyfriend. It is mutual.
   - If you have kept your sexual purity, this question may be very important, but if not, it may be irrelevant.
   - If she decides to lie to you about her sexual purity, I guess you'll find out on your first bridal night, because girls who are virgins release a lot of blood during their first sexual intercourse.

6. *Has she ever had an abortion?*
   - This is a very personal question that will determine how honest she is and whether she will hide anything personal from you in marriage.
   - If she had an abortion, find out if she had more than one. Or why she decided to have an abortion.

7. *What is her current relationship with the Lord?*
   - Again, this is a simple question to ask, but it is critical because many marriages have failed because one or both spouses were not fully rooted and grounded in their daily walk with the Lord.

8. *Does she have any medical issues or is she taking any serious prescriptions?*

- Because of our advanced medical technology and the wide range of prescription drugs that are readily available, we can become oblivious to the possibility that the person we love is on serious medications and has serious medical issues.
- Because medical issues differ from person to person, you must learn in great detail if your prospective bride-to-be could be an unstable wife, mother, and lover as a result of the hard-core prescription drugs she is currently taking.
- Some medical conditions are short-term, while others are chronic.

9. ***Is she willing to have children and how many?***
   - Despite the fact that this is a no-brainer question, you would be surprised at how many girls/women are very reserved in this area because they are either afraid or do not want their physical body and certain body parts to change as a result of pregnancy.
   - Regardless of the fact that bringing a new human being into this world is one of God's commandments and blessings, some people will not have more than one child. As much as this is a personal decision for the husband and wife, I would like to sincerely encourage both of you to consider having at least two children, as this will allow your children to form a much-needed bond with each other and with their parents.
   - Furthermore, having at least two children is highly recommended because having one child places that child in a sphere of being spoiled, which results in that child being self-centered. Moreover, the mother frequently becomes overly attached to their child and,

as a result, begins to neglect her husband. And it is for this reason that I have included one of the questions: Is she/he the only child?

- Yes, there are medical reasons why some people cannot or should not have children, which is completely understandable, but I want to address a deeper issue because I have personally observed how those who were the only child in the family were depressed, lonely, and one person once told me, "Stan, I hate my father and mother for not giving me a baby brother or a baby sister."

10. Is she willing to let go of her mother and father?

- For some, this may appear to be a childish question, but there is a reason why the Almighty God stated that a man must leave his parents' house in order to unite as one with his wife. This concept also applies to women.
- It is difficult for the daughter to let go of her mother (if she is still alive), especially if she is the only daughter or child.
- I know marriages that have failed and many marriages that are on the rocks because the wife did not fully let go of her mother and allowed her mother into their marriage, bedroom, and family affairs.
- Yes, there are some mother-in-laws who are controlling and want to know everything, but if the daughter (wife) is wise, she will keep her mother at a distance.
- Having said that, if the wife does not let go of her mother, they will never truly join together and become one as God intended for this marriage union

to be. The husband will be extremely frustrated as a result of this. And this will lead to multiple arguments and fights, possibly leading to a divorce.

The questions above are deep and serious, and they will most likely make any guy uncomfortable because we are not used to asking tough questions, especially to the person we love. Nonetheless, these questions may steer your heart in a different direction, causing you to notice certain red flags that will allow you to avoid proposing to her. Or, at the very least, to wait a little longer.

"IT'S BETTER TO KNOW CERTAIN THINGS AHEAD OF TIME THAN TO BITTERLY DISCOVER THEM LATER IN LIFE."

RATED "R" RECOMMENDATIONS

- Before you say, "I do," seriously consider all of your options and conduct thorough research on the person who is proposing to you.
- Before you propose to the love of your life, be prepared to ask probing questions, and roll up your sleeves to learn as much as you can about your prospective bride.
  Before getting married, it's a good idea to practice asking intelligent questions.
- Asking tough questions could unlock many secrets.

15

THE SIGNIFICANCE OF BEING SINGLE

Have you ever heard someone say, "I miss the good old days!" Or "I wish I was younger again." Alternatively, "If I could go back in time and be single again, I would have made different decisions in my life." All the statements above contain some truth, but they stray far from reality, which is that you and I cannot go back in time and make ourselves younger.

The concept of staying young or attempting to look and feel younger is not new, but the thoughts that constantly bombarded millions of people around the world about their younger years or how life was drastically different when they were single are. This same idea has gripped the hearts and minds of many married couples who have divorced or had unnecessary struggles in their marriage because they did not fully comprehend the significance of being single. And the late Dr. Myles Munroe made the following powerful and thought-provoking statement: "It is more important to be single than to be married. And that is why most people get a divorce. Because they were never single."[1]

That's a profound statement! What exactly does it mean? Should you not get married? No! The valuable lesson here is to make the most of your single years and to ensure that you are mature enough before jumping into marriage. And here's a rundown of some of the advantages and significance of being single:

- *More free time.*
- *More flexibility to doing what Gods wants you to do in this season of your life.*
- *Less responsibilities (no family, no spouse, no children).*
- *While you are single, you have much valuable time to personally develop yourself.*
- *While you are single you have a vast opportunity to generate and to establish a solid financial foundation.*

That was only a brief overview of some of the benefits of being unmarried. And in this chapter, I wanted to emphasize the importance of choosing your friends wisely, managing your time wisely, and first discovering your God-given purpose.

CHOOSE YOUR FRIENDS WISELY

Friends play a vital role in our lives, and the Bible is full of positive verses that emphasize the importance of having good friends in your life. And, while you are still single, it is critical that you surround yourself with Godly friends who have a credible character and are interested in your success in all aspects of your life. And the Apostle Paul challenges us with these strong words: "Do not be misled: 'Bad company corrupts good character.'"[2]

What Apostle Paul is doing is challenging us all to be aware and alert of our surroundings, particularly the type of friends we have in our lives. Because your friends will either enhance or detract from your personal character. And if you know your kingdom purpose, you will be able to sort through and eliminate every person who enters your life.

Additionally, your friends should be very interested in your success and future, and true friends will do everything they can to ensure that you are not engaging in sexual immorality or inappropriate behavior with girls. And if these friends are ungodly or unbelievers, I strongly advise you to make new friends who love the Lord and abide in the fear of the Lord. These few good friends will assist you in living a meaningful life as a single person. And keep in mind that your life's purpose cannot be fulfilled or accomplished by yourself; it will always necessitate the assistance, guidance, wisdom, and mentorship of those around you.

"CHOOSE YOUR FRIENDS IN ACCORDANCE WITH YOUR PURPOSE."

MANAGE YOUR TIME WISELY

Time is a valuable commodity and asset, and it is especially valuable when you are single. In chapter three of Ecclesiastes, King Solomon provides a unique timeline, stating that everything has its own season and time to fulfill a specific purpose. This is also true when you are single for a season; this time is special, but it is also a season. That is, you will not alwayss be single; this is just a phase.

So, managing your time is critical and will contribute to your personal growth and the development of healthy habits. When you are single, you have the time to complete your education, start a business, build a solid financial portfolio, travel, and, most importantly, be used by God to go on mission trips or other ministry opportunities.

Managing your time wisely will also help you develop the necessary character and discipline that you will require when you marry. Because if you can develop healthy habits and disciplines while you are single, it will only benefit your marriage.

"WHOEVER CONTROLS OR PLANS YOUR TIME WILL ALSO BE THE ONE WHO DESIGNS YOUR FUTURE. SO, DO NOT JUST SIMPLY EXIST, BUT LIVE A LIFE OF PURPOSE."

FIRST DISCOVER YOUR GOD-GIVEN PURPOSE

When you are single, you have much more time on your hands and more opportunities to do things that you would not have if you were married or had children. And it is essential that you discover and understand your God-given purpose for life during this one season of your life. So, what is purpose? The thing that captures your heart and mind's attention. Or your purpose is what God has called you to do and fulfill on this earth.

Again, why is knowing your purpose so vital? Because finding your purpose is the discovery of the original reason for your birth and existence. Furthermore, God created you specifically to solve a problem on this planet. And the potential of your kingdom purpose is limitless, but it is entirely dependent on you and how much you allow your purpose to be released. Your purpose, on the other hand, will not appear out of nowhere. You must discover it! You must cultivate it! And you have to release it!

Furthermore, the more you grasp God's promises in your life, the clearer your calling and purpose on this planet will become. Knowing your kingdom purpose will provide you with a clear objective, an action plan, and a stronger vision. Additionally, your kingdom purpose will not only make you unique, but it will also set you apart from the crowd.

So, being single isn't the main issue for single people; it's the fear of being alone. And there is a significant difference between being single and being alone, but many people confuse the two, prompting them to enter the realm of marriage before they are fully mature. And the sooner you understand your God-given purpose, the less alone you will feel.

"FIRST DISCOVER YOUR KINGDOM PURPOSE AND WHO YOU ARE IN CHRIST, THEN MAKE THE BOLD STEP TOWARDS MARRIAGE."

RATED "R" RECOMMENDATIONS

- Being single is a one-of-a-kind season that God purposefully designed, so make the most of it.
- Not knowing your true purpose and existence on this earth is one of the symptoms of boredom, depression, fear, or misery. So, while you're still single, figure out what your God-given purpose is.
- Knowing your God-given purpose will aid you in your dating, relationship, and marriage seasons.
- While you are still single, time will be a valuable commodity that you must guard and value.
- Surround yourself with friends who are willing to go out of their way to see you succeed and be blessed in life.

16

THE DIVORCE PANDEMIC

In a typical wedding ceremony, the couple exchanges vows, and one of the most common lines in the vow is: "Till death do us part." And, as profound as this is, it appears that in most cases, this phrase has no power. Unfortunately, it is not death that separates a married couple, but a divorce and every so often, a bitter and treacherous divorce.

The CDC has reported that in 2019, there were 2,015,603 marriages, and 746,971 divorces just in the Unites States.[1] The divorce rate among Christians is no different. This is a true pandemic that is not improving. And in this chapter, I'd like to challenge you to strengthen your spiritual foundation while you're still single, as well as warn you that once you're married, there should be no return label included in your wedding package.

BUILD A STROND SPIRITUAL FOUNDATION WHILE YOU ARE STILL SINOLE

So far, I've attended approximately 150 weddings in my lifetime. Each wedding was one-of-a-kind and special in its own way. And, while a wedding day is usually one of the most joyful days of a person's life, I've also seen a number of these same couple's divorce and marriages fall apart over the years. So, what exactly happened?

With the opportunity to know the majority of these newlywed couples, I began to investigate and investigate what caused these couples to divorce. And we frequently believe that it is unfaithfulness, betrayal, distrust, or unhealthy habits that deplete the family finances. All of the preceding is true, but in my observation, I began to see the main root cause of divorce, which is that the couple did not have a strong and healthy spiritual foundation before they married. In other words, their personal relationship with Jesus was primarily limited to Sunday services, with no personal prayer life, getting rooted and grounded in God's Word, or becoming involved in their local church as they discovered and understood their God-given purpose.

Having said that, Apostle Paul once again provides sound wisdom in this area, pointing out some truths for those who are still single: "I want you to be free from the concerns of this life. An unmarried man spends his time doing the Lord's work and thinking how to please Him. But a married man has to think about his earthly responsibilities and how to please his wife."[2] And Apostle Paul had the similar instructions for the woman: "The unmarried woman cares about the things of the Lord, that she may be holy both in body and in spirit. But she who is married cares about the things of the world – how she may please *her* husband."[3]

Building a strong and healthy spiritual foundation while single is not an option; it is a must. You don't want to enter into marriage with a cracked or weak spiritual foundation that can't support your family. And your heavenly Father will guarantee you a healthy and vibrant marriage if He becomes your rock on which you build your life.

"THE HEALTH OF YOUR MARRIAGE AND FUTURE FAMILY WILL BE DETERMINED BY THE STRENGTH OF YOUR SPIRITUAL FOUNDATION."

THE DIVORCE PANDEMIC

I've yet to hear from a divorced person that their divorce was easy or that it wasn't so bad. And, by God's grace, I've been married to an amazing and beautiful woman of God for twenty years as I write this book. But I could only imagine the heartache and sleepless nights that people go through as a result of divorce, as I have witnessed a good number of them in my life.

The following are some of the most common symptoms that arise in the life of a divorced person:

- *Anger and bitterness*
- *Hatred towards their divorced spouse*
- *Sleepless nights*

- *Anger and bitterness towards God*
- *A measure of jealousy knowing that another man/woman is currently living with them*
- *A feeling of guilt that your son or daughter is being raised by another stepparent*
- *Depression and anxiety*
- *Unhealthy eating habits*
- *Substance abuse*
- *Unhealthy dating relationships*
- *A rapid spiritual collapse*

As much as all of the preceding may appear dark and devastating, I have also witnessed individuals who had gone through a divorce but made a strong decision to grab a hold of God and follow Him wholeheartedly, which resulted in their accelerated emotional healing, peaceful sleeping, and the beginning of a brand-new chapter in their life.

Years ago, I recall speaking with a Christian man who told me that he had recently divorced because another man had enticed his wife away from him. And he was already plotting a way to kill this guy in his rage and bitterness. But God intervened, and the next day I prayed for him to receive inner healing and to fully forgive this man and his ex-wife, which he did as tears streamed down his face like a waterfall.

Divorce is cruel, it is nasty, and it can leave lifelong scars that many people do not recover from. Divorce was never in God's original plan, but the enemy of our soul has discovered flaws and weaknesses in our selfish human nature, and he knows that if he can destroy the original family covenant, everything else will crumble like dominoes. But, my friend, this should not be the case, and I want to challenge you, whether you are single or married, to become fully rooted and grounded in His Word, in His presence, and in the right Godly environment. And this will create a heavenly barrier around you and your marriage.

"DIVORCE WAS NEVER GOD'S OPTION, AND IT SHOULD NOT BE YOURS."

A RETURN LABEL IS NOT INCLUDED

Almost anything we buy can be returned and we will receive a full refund. And this is a great option to have because sometimes items we purchase do not meet our expectations, or the photo we saw online was deceiving in comparison to what you may be holding in your hands right now. However, this luxurious option is not available in marriage. In other words, when you get married, your wedding package will not include a return label, allowing you to easily return your bride to her parents or have her drop you off at your mother's house.

As much as I'm being facetious here, I want you to take this truth seriously. A couple usually exchanges vows on their wedding day, and one of the most common phrases in these vows is "This day I take." Nobody ever says, "This day I will return!" And during the wedding vows, the couple usually shares some of the most precious and intimate words, which I have seen many times where the groom tears up, the bride's make-up and mascara wash out, or even the guy's cry. This is a special moment, but for many couples, these special moments have already passed them by like vapor.

My wife and I had endless conversations about our future, how many children we wanted to have, and the possibility of divorce when we first married. And we both decided that divorce is not an option on our table, and that whatever difficult seasons or difficult decisions we may face in the near future, divorce is not an option. Have we had a difficult season? There were plenty of them! Were these trying times because our marriage or relationship was failing? No! We went through many difficult times in our marriage, just like any other normal couple, and divorce was never even on our radar.

Dear single person, if you have not yet married, seriously evaluate your life, your heart, and the seriousness of marriage before making those powerful marriage commitments at the wedding alter. And if you're married and going through a difficult season or have been through treacherous valleys in your marriage, I'd like to encourage and remind you of your original marriage vows and how much in love you both were on your special day. Furthermore, embrace this profound principle: once you both said, "I do," at the altar, there was no turning back, only moving forward with God's help and fulfilling His divine purpose for your life, marriage, and family.

"MARRIAGE IS A GIFT FROM ABOVE, FROM YOUR HEAVENLY FATHER, AND THIS GIFT WAS GIVEN WITHOUT ANY RETURN LABELS. BECAUSE GOD MAKES NO MISTAKES."

RATED "R" RECOMMENDATIONS

- Divorce should not be an option before or after marriage.
- When the time comes to plan your wedding, make sure you and your fiancé agree that your wedding package will not include a return label.
- While you are still single, make it a priority to establish a solid spiritual foundation.
- Divorce is one of the most traumatic events in a person's life.
- If love is the superglue that holds two people together, then divorce is the knife that pierces their hearts.
- If you don't want to experience a divorce, then stay sexually pure before and during your marriage.

17

WOLVES IN SHEEP'S CLOTHING!

I had the greatest honor of serving as a youth pastor for ten years. During these priceless years, I have been tremendously blessed and have learned many valuable lessons. And in the process, I've seen so many young hearts change and transform. And I've also seen many people struggle with insecurities, habitual sins, and broken relationships. And as I reflect on those years, I have fond memories of how the Lord was able to use me to impact and touch the lives of those precious hearts, as well as witnessing on social media how many of them have already married, had children, relocated geographically, and have successful businesses.

Having had the honor and privilege of serving as a youth pastor, I fully understand the critical role that a youth pastor plays in the local church, as they are the primary person through whom the Lord influences the younger generation. Having said that, not everyone is qualified to take this special baton and become the seasonal leader to guide the youth toward their kingdom purpose. And in this one-of-a-kind chapter, I want to challenge every pastor and parent to understand the critical role that a youth pastor plays in the lives of youth and your son and daughter by discussing a youth pastor's resume.

THE TRANSPARENT RESUME OF A YOUTH PASTOR

We are all too familiar with the concept of a resume, which is sometimes accompanied by a cover letter. The basic idea behind a resume is to give the employer or hiring manager a quick glimpse of the applicant in order to determine if they have the necessary qualifications for that specific open position. And if the employer does not see what they prefer, the application with the resume is frequently discarded. And there was a time in my life when I was desperate for work, and I filled out over 400 applications and spent hundreds of hours applying for jobs over a two-and-a-half-year period. And most employers rejected my application because I did not have a bachelor's degree, despite having extensive personal experience.

Now, the whole concept of hiring has drastically shifted, due to many who choose not to work, or because many who do possess a bachelors or master's degree have a lot of brain knowledge but possess too little practical life skills and the employers are often struggling with re-teaching and re-training these highly educated graduates.

So, when it comes to hiring a youth pastor, any church should look beyond their experience, beyond their spiritual qualifications, and even beyond the notion of how much they love the Lord. What exactly do I mean by all of this? We are witnessing an unprecedented number of youth pastors who have committed heinous sexual acts with one of their youth members, or who live a double life, or who are secretly addicted to pornography, or who are not married but are sexually active with their girlfriend.

All of the preceding frequently has to do with the youth pastors' former sinful life, from which they presumably repented. And I'd like to pose a few questions that might be useful to the pastor or the person in charge of overseeing the hiring process for new staff members:

Questions to consider during the interview:

1. ***Are they married?***
   - This is not required, but it is extremely beneficial in youth ministry.
   - If they are not married but are of the appropriate mature age, inquire as to what is stopping them from marrying.
2. ***If not married, is he/she a virgin?***
   - Despite the fact that this question may appear to be personal, it should not be overlooked.
   - If they are not a virgin, learn as much as you can about their previous relationships and lifestyle.
   - This is not intended to bring up their sinful past, but rather to shed some light on potential red flags.
3. ***Do they have a child out of wedlock?***
   - Again, this question is unique in many ways, but if they have a child out of wedlock, find out what their current situation is with their child.
4. ***Are the parents married or divorced?***

- This question will be extremely beneficial in understanding this potential youth pastor's upbringing and the type of family environment they grew up in.
  - Toxic or abusive environments leave a deep scar in a child's heart and mind, which can take years to heal, and this toxicity can be released in the youth ministry.

5. ***Has he/she been ever molested or raped?***
   - This is a deep and sensitive question that will make this person very uncomfortable.
   - Uncomfortable because it is unusual, or comfortable because you may strike a deeply hidden pain that this person has kept private for years.
   - If this person has experienced such trauma in the past, you as a pastor must be certain that they have fully healed and forgiven their perpetrator. However, if you have the opposite impression, I will then advise you that this person is not qualified to be a youth pastor.

6. ***What are their biblical views on LGBTQ, same sex marriage, dating, and relationships?***
   - This is not a theological question per say, but rather one to learn about this potential individual's views, beliefs, and biblical convictions.
   - ***Are they currently living with their parent or independently?***
   - This question, depending on their age, allows you to learn about their leadership abilities and personal life accountability.

7. ***Why do they want to be a youth pastor?***
   - This question is critical because it will allow you to truly discern their heart motive, whether they are

passionate about the younger generation or simply looking for a title and a steady paycheck.

- Furthermore, some take advantage of the youth pastoral position as a steppingstone to a higher position or simply to build their resume in order to apply in the near future with a prestige ministry or a well-known church.

The questions above are not meant to be binding, but rather to shed some light on who this person needs to be. Because the hearts of the youth are immature, naive, and very vulnerable, and the potential youth pastor needs to be the shepherd in their life rather than a hireling. Allow me to tickle your spiritual toes for a moment with this mind-boggling suggestion: what if every local church built their job description for a potential youth pastor with the following minimum qualifications:

- *You must have been a virgin before getting married.*
- *Prior to marriage, had no sex or any sexual activities.*
- *Dated no more than two individuals in their life.*
- *Was never on antidepressants, or struggled with thoughts of suicide.*
- *Does not come from a divorced family.*
- *Grew up with both biological parents.*
- *Was never incarcerated.*
- *Have no visible tattoos.*
- *Was not sexually molested (raped) by someone.*

I could imagine your eyes widening and your brows furrowing in disbelief. And, as much as there is truth in my suggestions above, this will never be written on a church's job posting because it would disqualify many potential candidates right away. Some of you reading this might easily put me in a legalistic box with the words "Beware, this person is a religious Pharisee."

My point is not to be legalistic or to judge these potential youth pastors, but fully recognizing that our heavenly Father is full of love, mercy, and forgiveness to anyone with any type of sinful background, but the point here is that we don't bother to include these necessary qualifications, knowing that this potential individual will be the spiritual shepherd to our son or daughter. Furthermore, such individuals (youth pastors) will appear hypocritical if they talk, preach, teach, or give sound advice on dating, relationships, sexual purity, or even marriage when they have not lived up to similar standards in their own lives.

Many credible companies and workplaces have high standards for hiring a much-needed qualified candidate, outlining in great detail what minimum qualifications this individual must have, and by doing so, they have already filtered out many who are unqualified or simply looking for a job with a good salary. So, why can't the body of Christ use similar criteria when hiring a potential youth pastor? Just an idea!

"BEING A LEADER IS A PERSONAL CHOICE BUT BEING ABLE TO SERVE IN THE LOCAL CHURCH IS AN HONOR."

WOLVES IN SHEEP'S CLOTHING

Jesus once warned His disciples about wolves in sheep's clothing, and this He was referring to the false prophets.[1] These wolves in sheep's clothing are not limited to false prophets, but to anyone who is deceived or controlled by demonic spirits, or who has a carnal agenda motivated by the spirit of this world.

In my years of ministry and as a Christian for over twenty years, I have heard much teaching and preaching about these types of wolves in sheep's clothing, and honestly, I had a narrowminded understanding of who would fall into this type of category, frequently believing that the devil would send his demonic agents to infiltrate local churches and allow deceptive teaching to cripple into the pulpit. All of the preceding is true, but it is not the crux of the problem. Until one day I was hit with a reality check that took my spiritual understanding to a whole new level.

In 2011, I was a youth pastor and one of the church leaders at a church I used to attend. We had a man in his early fifties who started coming to our weekly Sunday services and even our weekly youth services on Friday nights. This gentleman lived directly across the street from the church. This individual was distinguished by the fact that he was in a wheelchair. After learning about our local church, he began riding his wheelchair twice a week to attend our services.

This man appeared to love the Lord, based on my observations. In his speech, he was pleasant. He was well-versed in the Bible, and the people in our church seemed to like him. I've even hosted my young man's life group at his house. However, there were a couple of occasions when some of my worship team members began to express their discomfort by saying that this man would frequently arrive early to our Friday night youth service, while the worship team was rehearsing, and would sit in his wheelchair in the front row and sing along with the group, but some of the worship folks felt uncomfortable with this, saying, "It feels like he is constantly staring at us."

Being somewhat spiritually immature and naïve, I simply ignored it because this man made no inappropriate gestures or said or did anything out of the ordinary. Something happened a short time later that completely changed everything. One day, as we were doing our usual parking lot community outreach, a teenager from the local community saw this man in the wheelchair and approached one of our leaders, asking, "Why is this guy here?" "Do you have no idea who he is?" When this leader approached me, I discovered that this seemingly innocent-looking man in a wheelchair was a third-level sex offender.

Talk about cold chills coursing through my entire body. With some skepticism and disbelief about what I had just learned, I went on the computer later that day to do some research and find out more about this same man, who had been convicted of rape of a child and also had two accounts of assault and battery on a child. And because the law defines a level three sex offender as the most serious level, this is the most serious offence. Furthermore, research and statistics show that these offenders are more likely to commit the same offense again, which is why they are required by law to register so that the local community knows who they are and where they live.

I eventually shared this information with my pastor, and we met with other leaders and this man to discuss our main concern. And our concern was that he had never informed us of his criminal status, and that we as a church could have gotten ourselves into serious legal trouble because he freely attended our youth services and other venues where children were present. We asked him if he had fully repented of his dark and vicious deeds during our conversation, and he said, "yes." We asked him again if he believes he has been fully delivered from this demonic and lustful behavior, and he said, "yes."

And during our conversation, I felt in my heart that he had not fully repented and been delivered from his malevolent acts, and my pastor and other leaders felt the same way after our meeting. Anyway, after we expressed our concern, this man apologized, and we told him that from now on, he could only attend Sunday services and that he could never attend any youth, children, or festival events that we held. When we imposed these strict restrictions on him, he immediately responded, "Well, I will no longer attend this church." We then told him that we were not kicking him out and that we wanted to be there for him and help him, but he politely declined and immediately left our church grounds.

This one situation stood out as a powerful example of a wolf in sheep's clothing to me. But this isn't the end of the story. About six months before the whole thing became public, one of my friends had a dream in which he saw three animals: a wolf, a leopard, and a falcon. And in the dream, these animals were doing different things. The wolf was drinking clear water from a stream, the leopard was positioned in an attack mode, as if waiting to ambush its prey, and the falcon was tamed because it had its eye covered and would fly and land on the master's hand whenever the master whistled for it. And we spent months attempting to decipher or interpret this dream because it did not provide us with any peace.

Only after this situation with this man occurred, and shortly thereafter, did I receive an interpretation for my friend's dream. I can still recall the interpretation's specifics to this day. Here are the specifics:

- **The Wolf:** Was drinking fresh water from the stream.
  - Interpretation – *The wolf was symbolic to the power of lust and as the wolf was drinking the clean fresh water, this water was symbolic to innocence. This innocence represents the youth and the children in our local church.*
- **The Leopard:** Was postured in the attack mode.
  - Interpretation – *The leopard was symbolic to power and deception, and he hid itself from its prey. And the attack position that it is, was that this leopard was ready to attack its next victim.*
- **The Falcon:** Was had blinders on both of its eyes, and as soon as he heard the trainer/master call for it, right away it flew and landed on the trainers/master's hand.
  - Interpretation – *The falcon symbolized this man in the wheelchair who was still blinded by his perverse sins, and every time the trainer/master (the devil) called for him, he quickly obeyed his voice.*
  - *This final interpretation allowed all of us to know that this man was still bound by his sins, which was evident on his body language when we spoke with him and other vital factors.*

The situation described above may be unique to my personal experience, but it is not uncommon in the body of Christ, as these wolves come from a variety of backgrounds and have a variety of criminal records. And this is once again a vital importance for any pastor to be fully aware of who is or will shepherding their flock.

For about eight years, my family attended Free Chapel, the main campus, and during those years, we were tremendously blessed as our spirit man was stuffed to the brim with knowledge, wisdom, and exposure. And, because I had the opportunity to connect with many pastors and church leaders, I learned why Free Chapel was so successful and influential. And for about five of the eight years, my wife worked as a paid volunteer in the children's ministry department, and one thing we both learned was how seriously they took the idea of conducting criminal background checks.

Anyone interested in getting involved in the children's or youth ministries had to go through a background check. And, while this may not come as a surprise to some of you reading this, I have learned from one of the key pastors that they would sometimes spend thousands of dollars each month on background checks because the church is large, and they always need volunteers.

What is the key takeaway here? We should never take things for granted or be spiritually naive to the fact that this world is full of wolves in sheep's clothing, and just because someone says they love the Lord and even tithes consistently does not mean they are a trustworthy or even a true born-again Christian. This is also true in terms of dating, relationships, and marriage. Ask honest, and hard questions to get to know the other person.

"YOU CAN ALLEVIATE A LOT OF HEARTACHE IF YOU TAKE THE TIME TO GET TO KNOW THE OTHER PERSON."

RATED "R" RECOMMENDATIONS

- As a pastor, you must be deeply familiar with your church's leaders and ministers.
- As a parent, it is highly recommended that you understand who your local church's youth pastor is.
- As a teen, you should love and respect your youth pastor, but you should also be aware of who they are and pay attention to their speech, behavior outside of the church, and body language.
- To want to be used by God to serve others, particularly the younger generation, there is a requirement to live a sexually pure life.
- Asking the right questions may elicit a deceptive response but asking tough questions will reveal the truth.

18

I AM NOT FOR SALE!

Have you ever seen something you really wanted only to discover that it was not for sale? Perhaps you've even offered a large sum of money to someone to purchase an item that you'd been looking for a long time, only to be told, "Sorry, it's not for sale." Sure, disappointment set in, but you had to accept the reality of the situation at some point.

And in this unconventional chapter, I will discuss the importance of setting boundaries in your personal life, in dating, in a relationship, while engaged, and even when married. Many people choose to ignore the significance of boundaries, and as a result, they end up in a major wreck, just like someone who foolishly ignores the seatbelt in their vehicle, thinking they will be fine. So buckle up, my friend, because we're about to embark on another thrilling adventure.

YOU CAN'T TOUCH THIS!

One of the hit songs that we as teenagers jammed to when I was growing up was MC Hammer's "U Can't Touch This." And I'd like to take this opportunity to emphasize the significance of how much you value yourself, as well as how much you honor and value the opposite gender.

The act of flirting or fooling around with the opposite sex for the sake of amusement has dire and painful consequences. And, while it may be cool and acceptable among teenagers at school, the important question is where the limitations and boundaries to these lustful behaviors are. And, once again, Apostle Paul offers a unique warning to all readers when he says: "It is good for a man not to touch a woman."[1] He further explains that this type of behavior will lead to sexually immoral conduct.

Some people are shocked and amazed at how they ended up naked in bed having sex with someone they never intended to have sex with, or tragically, being raped by a guy or a group of guys at a party. All of the above are the results of what happened previously over a period of time when the girl would frequently dress very sexily, exposing her cleavage and other body ports, which naturally attracted the lustful appetites of guys. Furthermore, flirtation frequently involves touching one another, including private parts of the body. High school and college parties, where anything goes, are among the most dangerous.

I was once watching the news when I saw a mayor in Florida apologize on national television for the erratic and perverse behavior of the college students who flooded the beaches during spring break. Numerous rapes occurred that year, and some were having sexual orgies right on the beach while the rest cheered them on. And if you truly believe you are a born-again Christian, you must know when to say, "You can't touch this." If you don't set these strict boundaries, whether you're a guy or a girl, don't be surprised if someone tries to take advantage of you.

Here are some warning signs that you should be aware of when it comes to setting boundaries in friendships, dating, or relationships:

- If the guy easily touches you, especially in an inappropriate way, this is a sign that he has no respect for you and is not interested in you as a person, but he is looking forward to having sexual relations with you or is simply a pervert.
- If a guy or a girl freely offers you sex with them, run! I mean it in a literal sense. Run! Many people are drawn into a sexual or promiscuous lifestyle during these times. Again, stay away from such people.
- If a girl lustfully stares at you, not just glances at you, but deliberately stares at you, avoid that eye contact.
- If you believe your relationship is progressing too quickly, you should either stop seeing each other for a period of time or end it permanently.
- If a guy who could also be a friend uses loose sexual (supposedly complimenting) language towards you, he is not worthy of your friendship. These are not idle remarks; they demonstrate how he dishonors and disrespects you for who you are.
- If the person you're dating or in a serious relationship with listens to sexually perverse songs (lyrics), you should confront them about it, because these types of songs stimulate the mind with sexual thoughts, which will eventually lead to other sexually inappropriate behavior.

All of the examples above are straightforward and raw in their depictions, but they are all too real, and many precious hearts and lives have been broken and people have been destroyed. And the Book of Proverbs explains in detail how the appetite for sexual sin works. Let's take a closer look:

At the window of my house
I looked down through the lattice.
I saw among the simple,
I noticed among the young men,
a youth who had no sense.
He was going down the street near her corner,
walking along in the direction of her house
at twilight, as the day was fading,
as the dark of night set in.
Then out came a woman to meet him,
dressed like a prostitute and with crafty intent.
(She is unruly and defiant,
her feet never stay at home;
now in the street, now in the squares,
at every corner she lurks.)
She took hold of him and kissed him
and with a brazen face she said:
"Today I fulfilled my vows,
and I have food from my fellowship offering at home.
So I came out to meet you;
I looked for you and have found you!
I have covered my bed
with colored linens from Egypt.
I have perfumed my bed
with myrrh, aloes and cinnamon.
Come, let's drink deeply of love till morning;
let's enjoy ourselves with love!
-Proverbs 7:6-18 NIV

The previous passages pull no punches, stating unequivocally the power of lust and sexual appetites. And whether you're flirting or messing around with the opposite sex, you're playing with fire, and you'll get burned eventually. HIV and other deadly sexual diseases are rapidly spreading, and those who are affected are surprised because they supposedly used protection; however, those who choose to willfully engage in sexual sins have no protection and only open the door to judgment and punishment. And, as our bodies are the temple of the Holy Spirit, I wholeheartedly challenge you to live a life of holiness and purity, refusing to advertise yourself or your body for sexual exploits.

"IF YOU PLAY WITH SIN, YOU WILL BITTERLY REAP ITS LETHAL BITE."

BOUNDARIES ARE FOR YOUR PROTECTION

What exactly are boundaries? Boundaries are a type of barrier that imposes certain constraints or limitations. These boundaries are not intended to bind or imprison a person, but rather to guard and protect them. So, how does one establish practical boundaries while dating, in a relationship, during the engagement season, and even in marriage?

Our carnal human nature always wants to push everything to its limits, or to know how far we can go or how far that boundary limit is. This is also visible in small children who continue to explore the new world as if they are Christopher Columbus, and anyone who has been a parent knows that you can never take your eyes off your child, or they will get themselves into a big mess or possibly hurt themselves.

While this may be acceptable for children, as we grow older and mature, we all have that inner child who wants to see how far we can go and how much we can get away with. This same human instinct drives our selfish nature to disregard the importance of boundaries, and as a result, we face dire consequences as a result of our rash and self-centered decisions.

You must have boundaries whether you are single and dating or in a serious relationship for your own protection and the protection of the person you love. Boundaries are not rules and regulations, but rather a red light that will keep you safe during your dating or relationship season. And the fear of the Lord is one of the best boundaries that anyone can have, as it will protect both of you in your relationship and give you the knowledge and wisdom to know that your body is not for sale, but is the temple of the Holy Spirit, and your body belongs to the Lord while you are single, and your body will now belong to your spouse when you get married.

"BOUNDARIES IN YOUR LIFE ARE LIKE METAL GUARDRAILS ON THE EDGE OF A CLIFF, KEEPING YOU FROM DESTROYING YOUR FUTURE."

RATED "R" RECOMMENDATIONS

- Because your body does not belong to you, but to the Lord, you should never offer it for sexual exploits outside of marriage, nor should you allow someone to inappropriately touch you.
- "I am not for sale," should be the mindset when you are single and when you get married.
- Create healthy boundaries in your life when you are single and especially when you get married.
- If your boyfriend purposely touches you inappropriately, you should end the relationship right away.
- Honor and value yourself and your physical body. And as you do, you will not allow others to inappropriately touch you.

19

TRY BEFORE YOU BUY

We've all bought something and then returned it for various reasons at some point. And I recently purchased an electric leaf blower that I was dissatisfied with, so I returned it to the store after cleaning it off of all of the dust. And while having this type of option or privilege is extremely beneficial in many ways, but does the same concept apply to dating, relationships, sex, and marriage? In other words, I can try before I buy!

And the obvious answer is no! When it comes to dealing with another human being, especially when feelings, emotions, and affection are involved, it is not the same as purchasing a thing that has no feelings or emotions, using it, and then returning it. You will not hurt these things feelings if you use and return it. When you are involved with another human being, however, this is not the case. Humans have too many feelings, too many emotions, and they do hurt when they are used and exploited. And in this chapter, I'd like to emphasize that dating, sex, and marriage are not experiments, but rather serious matters that should not be taken lightly. And that your personal testimony is extremely valuable.

DATING IS A SERIOUS DECISION NOT AN EXPERIMENT

The real questions are, "How many boyfriends or girlfriends do you have to go through before you find the right one?" Or "How long do you have to date someone for in order to be certain that this is the one?" The answers may differ depending on the individual and their personal dating belief system. But, regardless of how we approach the concept of dating, we must understand that it is a serious decision, not an experiment.

Knowing your seasons and being willing to step into a serious relationship, which will eventually lead to marriage, is one way to approach dating seriously, but if you are not ready for such a pathway, my honest recommendation is not to have a boyfriend/girlfriend or date anyone. As simple as this may seem on my end, it will keep you more focused on God and your personal relationship with Jesus without being distracted, as I have already discussed the significance of being single in the previous chapter. Finally, you do not want to position yourself to potentially move from one relationship to another, as this will wear you out emotionally and spiritually.

"DATING OR COURTING ALLOWS YOU TO GET TO KNOW SOMEONE MORE CLOSELY, BUT IT IS NOT AN OPPORTUNITY TO WASTE YOUR VALUABLE TIME."

SEX IS A GIFT FROM GOD NOT AN EXPERIMENT

Again, sex or a sexual relationship is not a quick meal that you order from a drive-through simply because you're hungry. Our sexuality is sacred and must be preserved for our spouse and only our spouse. However, if you choose to use this gift as a test for your lustful desires, the consequences will be severe. Furthermore, it has been a deception among many who believe they can live a promiscuous lifestyle as much as they want and then run to Jesus. This would be fantastic if you did run to Jesus, who has the power to deliver you from your sexually immoral lifestyle, but the more you engage in the sexually immoral lifestyle, the worse the consequences will be.

Another thing to consider is that men and women are wired differently when it comes to sex. The men are motivated by what they see, while the women are captivated by what they hear. All it takes for any guy with raging hormones and a high testosterone level to only look at pretty girls, or get fixated on her breast, visible cleavage, or smooth legs, to only then fall under a magical spell that begins to position their inner appetite as a lion slowly creeping towards its prey, with the ultimate goal being to satisfy that inner appetite with what their eyes are looking at.

Of course, it may appear that all guys are perverts, but this is not the case because not every guy is perverted in their mind; this is simply to demonstrate how guys are wired differently. Whereas sex may not be a big deal for a girl in a relationship, it is for the majority of guys. On the other hand, the girls get a lot of pleasure and satisfaction when their boyfriend compliments them on how they look or how they dress, and then adds flowers, a box of chocolates for Valentine's Day, and fancy dinners to that, which results in her becoming very open to him, where she just surrenders to him completely and allows her boyfriend to have sexual intercourse with her, even though that was something she never intended to do.

And the big issue here is that knowing how God wired guys and girls puts sex on the shelf of Spencer's Gifts, as something erotic, sexy, and lustful, rather than knowing and understanding that sex is a gift from God, not a mere experiment or something to fulfill your lustful desires because you can't control your raging hormones.

Additionally, our current culture has degraded and continues to degrade the true purpose and meaning of what sex is, and as the younger generation is constantly bombarded with this false narrative, we as parents and the body of Christ are fulfilling damage control, while we need to become frontrunners in teaching our children and youth that sex is not an experiment, but an awesome gift from God, which has been designed within a marriage covenant, which carries with it many blessings.

"SEX IS A GIFT FROM GOD, AND IT HAS TREMENDOUS VALUE AND WORTH, WHICH SHOULD NOT BE WASTED ON THOSE WHO ARE NOT YOUR SPOUSE."

MARRIAGE IS A COVENANT NOT AN EXPERIMENT

As I previously stated in the divorce pandemic chapter, once married, there is no return label, and you must only hold on to your married partner until death separates you. And I wanted to emphasize that marriage is a covenant, not an experiment. With our rapidly changing culture, it appears normal to divorce simply because you don't get along or don't see each other as compatible any longer.

When we carefully read through the history of the Israelites in the Old Testament, we see that God was strict with His warning to His chosen people, telling them that they could not intermarry with people from other nations or cultures and that they had to keep their bloodline pure. And when the Israelites disobeyed, God punished them, and one of the ways they could repent was to divorce their foreign-born spouses.

God's actions may have been harsh, but He knew what He was doing. With that said, marriage is sacred in the eyes of our Creator, and it is also a covenant with the same value as the covenant we have with Him through His son, Jesus Christ. This covenant has specific meaning, accountability, and obligations. Jesus has already done everything on His part; now it is our turn to be faithful and fully committed to serving Him. This is also true in the case of a marriage covenant, where God has orchestrated everything, and it is now our responsibility to fulfill our accountability. However, not in a contractual sense, as any contract can become null and void.

"MARRIAGE IS A SACRED GIFT SPECIALLY CRAFTED BY THE LOVING HANDS OF OUR HEAVENLY FATHER, WHICH BRINGS HIM GREAT JOY AND PLEASURE IN RETURN."

TRY BEFORE YOU BUY

Those of us who shop at Costco on a regular basis enjoy the opportunity to try or test out a food product that is being promoted by one of the staff, and if you are hungry, you will boldly grab two portions. And if we were walking through a mall or a fair and someone offered us a free sample, we would not hesitate to accept it. This same ideology has been ingrained in the hearts and minds of today's youth when it comes to dating, relationships, and sex. And the ideology is to "try before you buy." Try having sex with someone to see if you're compatible! See how far your relationship can go! And, from a man's point of view, if you can score a one-night stand, you are a true man!

Trying a food item to see if it appeals to your tastebuds is not the same as having sex with someone to see if they are a good match for you. And while it is normal to test drive a new car to see if it will fit your lifestyle, it is not the same as entering into a sexual relationship with someone outside of marriage to see if they will be a good fit for someone you may potentially marry!

The deluded thinking of going from one partner to another or one boyfriend/girlfriend to another to see which one is the best fit for your lustful passions will only lead you down a path of pain, agony, heartaches, depression, and sleepless nights.

Furthermore, the deception of thinking that you will gain more experience by dating more people or having more sex has been the pill that many have already swallowed, which gave them a very nauseous feeling and produced the opposite effect, which was a bad experience from which many have not recovered. And, typically, your first dating experience will imprint that experience as a template in your subconscious, as will your first sexual intercourse, if you lusted after someone in order to have sex with them, then that will become one's fixed mindset about sex.

Again, positioning your thinking of testing out a guy or a girl to determine if they are the best fit for you is dangerous, and could have long-term damaging consequences, leading many to cry in bitterness at night, substance abuse, and, in some cases, suicide. Choose to place your heart and desires in the hands of your heavenly Father, who knows what is best for you and will direct your steps toward a healthy relationship and a blessed marriage at the right time and in the right season.

"IT IS MORE VALUABLE TO TRUST IN THE LORD AND HIS WILL FOR YOUR LIFE THAN TO PLAY WITH FIRE, WHICH WILL EVENTUALLY BURN YOU."

THE POWER OF A PERSONAL TESTIMONY

Everyone has a unique personal life testimony of who they were and what the good Lord did for them as their life was transformed by the power of the cross and the washing away of our sins by the power of Jesus' blood. And I've heard incredible testimonies throughout my life, some of which will leave you speechless, while others will make the hairs on the back of your neck stand on end as to what the individual went through and how the Lord rescued them from the pits of hell. But I've also noticed a disheartening pattern in which more than 95 percent of the testimonies were based on people making bad decisions and delving deep into the world and its lusts, but only a very small handful of people who never went into the world or never tasted the world's lustful appetites.

These people aren't any better than the rest, but the main difference is that they chose to focus on the Lord and a deeper relationship with Jesus, which kept their heart, mind, and thoughts focused on the relationship with the lover of their soul rather than creating a relationship with the enemy of their soul. One of these people happens to be my lovely wife. However, I have the opposite testimony in which I went deep into the world. So, why is it that we rarely hear of testimonies of those who have consistently remained faithful to the Lord?

Another sobering thought is why do we rejoice and celebrate those who have been through hell and high water, but rarely acknowledge those who have not? Or why have we made it acceptable that everyone must live the worldly life of a typical prodigal son and then return to the heavenly Father? This should not be the case, and we as the body of Christ must raise the standards of holy living much higher in order to have many more powerful testimonies of those who did not succumb to the world's lustful appetites.

Finally, consider the following sobering questions: "Which is preferable: for a spouse to remain faithful throughout the marriage, or to commit adultery and then, with sincere bitter tears, ask their spouse for forgiveness, which the spouse forgives out of love?" Or "What makes more sense, to be in a car accident while buckled up and suffer minor injuries, or to suffer broken bones and serious injuries because your seatbelt was not fastened?" Or "You become pregnant unexpectedly as a teen and suffer with the guilt of aborting the child, or becoming pregnant while married and having your first child at the right time with the right person, your husband?"

The list of these types of questions could go on forever, but they are real and heart wrenching. Many people wish they could turn back time or undo the harm they have done to themselves, but we all know that turning back the tide of time is impossible. Yes, our heavenly Father's love and forgiveness are amazing, but it is also wonderful to remain in His mercy, grace, protection, and divine purpose.

"ALLOW YOUR PERSONAL TESTIMONY TO BECOME A CREDIBLE EXAMPLE TO OTHERS OF HOW IT IS POSSIBLE TO LIVE A SEXUALLY PURE LIFE AND MARRY AS A VIRGIN."

RATED "R" RECOMMENDATIONS

- Outside of a marriage covenant, it is not worth experimenting with any form of sexual behavior, my friend. Period!
- Dating is a serious business, not just a fun weekend activity.
- Sex is a divine gift from God, not a means of mere entertainment.
- Marriage is a lifelong covenant, not a contract that can be broken.
- It is entirely up to you to decide what kind of testimony or testimonies you want in your life. Because of God's love and forgiveness, all testimonies are powerful, but certain testimonies will have a far greater impact.

20

WE NEED MORE ROLE MODELS

One key component of any local church is to have credible and passionate mentors, spiritual fathers, and mothers who are willing to invest their personal time in discipling and equipping others, as these individuals serve as much-needed Godly role models. And a *role model* is defined as: A person whose behavior, example, or success is or can be emulated (imitated or mirrored) by others, especially by the younger people, as this person becomes a mentor to others.[1]

Role models are life coaches and mentors who want to guide others through their life journeys and personal self-discoveries. And in this critical chapter, I want to sound the trumpet loudly for kingdom role models to emerge, so that they can coach, mentor, and disciple the younger generation and married couples, so that we can have healthy marriages, healthy relationships, and healthy churches. "Healthy marriages will make healthy churches, and healthy churches will be able to have greater kingdom impact in their local community," as the saying goes.

COACH, MENTOR, AND DISCIPLE THE YOUNGER GENERATION

When I lived in Massachusetts, I led a weekly guy's group comprised of high school and college-aged students. This was an awesome group where we did life together by studying the Word, talking about guy issues, and tackling some of life's most difficult questions. We also went camping, hiking, and had many backyard firepit conversations.

And when I moved to the peachy state of Georgia, I wanted to start another guy's group for a while, and years later, I did start a new batch of young men I call Young Guns. Why devote your time to young men or young women? The answer is extremely simple! They are desperate for someone to share their life with as they navigate their teenage or young adulthood, where their hormones are raging, and they have a million tough and curious questions to ask someone.

And, by being that much-needed role model, you are automatically disciplining them rather than babysitting them, because the true essence of discipleship is not handing out spiritual pajamas but equipping every born-again believer with God's armor. And, as the body of Christ, we have done a good job of converting people, but we have very few solid and stable disciples, because converting people will give you church members, but discipling people so they will know their God-given

151

identity and purpose will give you kingdom ambassadors, who will boldly represent the King and His kingdom.

What I've discovered over the years is that there is an inner cry within the younger generation for people from their local churches to step up and roll up their sleeves and be that much needed role model to them. And one powerful truth to consider is that the younger generation is full of kingdom potential, which is dormant within their hearts and spirit man. And it is often necessary for a selfless individual, who is usually older and more mature, to enter the lives of these precious individuals and serve as a role model.

"THE YOUNGER GENERATION IS EAGERLY WAITING FOR MATURE AND CREDIBLE CHRISTIANS TO STEP FORWARD AS KINGDOM ROLE MODELS."

COACH, MENTOR, AND DISCIPLE OTHER COUPLES

There is a greater need than ever for credible Godly couples to take up the mantle of becoming coaches and mentors by discipling other couples, particularly engaged and newlywed couples. This became abundantly clear when my family and my best friend's family transitioned into another church family at the beginning of 2021. And in one conversation with a group of Godly married men, my friend expressed a strong desire to work with married couples, and before he could finish, the guys reacted with joy, enthusiasm, and a question about when he plans to launch this group.

In a nutshell, these married men began to express their concern that the church is overlooking this critical area where couples are looking to be mentored and desperately seeking wise counsel from credible couples willing to invest in their marriage. Soon after, my dear friend started this couple's life group, and the results were amazing.

Naomi did an excellent job mentoring Ruth, sharing her wisdom and guidance, paving the way for Ruth, an outsider, to marry a wealthy and Godly man named Boaz. And it's especially powerful when a godly couple can mentor another couple or a group of couples. And the Bible provides us with a good verse to demonstrate the importance of mentoring others: "As iron sharpens iron, so one person sharpens another."[2]

Those who believe that marriage is always a Disney World experience are delusory, and the right mentor in your life will be able to teach you to grow deep and strong roots, allowing you to withstand all of the tests and trials in marriage and in life. And it will take another seasoned and credible couple to mentor another younger couple; this is, in my opinion, one of the best ways to do it, but there are also other ways that couples can be mentored.

Any local church that focuses on coaching, mentoring, and discipling couples has a much better chance of having healthy and strong marriages, and healthy marriages only add value to that local church. And healthy marriages will naturally reproduce healthy marriages, and as new families join that local body, they will be heavily influenced by these other couples.

"SUCCESSFUL MENTORING IS LIKE A TANGO DANCE IN WHICH THE MENTOR GUIDES THE MENTEE STEP BY STEP WHILE THEY BOTH CULTIVATE A STRONG RAPPORT AND PARTNERSHIP."

KINGDOM ROLE MODELS PLEASE ARISE!

To say that anyone can become a role model is true, but to say that everyone should become a role model should cause us to pause for a moment and reconsider. In a nutshell, our local church and the body of Christ could benefit from more kingdom role models, but the harsh reality is that not everyone is qualified to be that Godly role model. In what way?

One of the ongoing challenges for any and every local church is a lack of approved individuals. Please make a note of this! I did not say that local churches do not have enough people who want to help but not enough approved people. What exactly does this mean? When Apostle Paul was writing his second letter to his young protégé Timothy, he said: "Be diligent to present yourself approved to God, a worker who does not need to be ashamed, rightly dividing the word of truth."[3]

The word *approved* is defined as: *to speak or think favorably of; allowed, authorized, endorsed, permitted, chosen, proven, and validated.*[4] And it was with this same word that the Apostle Paul challenged Timothy to present himself approved to God. This is also true for anyone who wishes to mentor or disciple others.

Again, the responsibility of being a role model to others is crucial, and it also carries a high caliber of responsibilities and qualifications, which is why, more than ever before, every local church and the body of Christ as a whole needs true kingdom role models to emerge and take their rightful place as they will become the type of spiritual fathers and mothers in their local churches, particularly to the younger generation.

"A TRUE MENTOR IS ABLE TO TAKE THEIR MENTEE WHO LOOKS LIKE A ROUGH AND A RUGGED LOOKING ROCK AND SHAPE THEM INTO A VALUABLE DIAMOND."

RATED "R" RECOMMENDATIONS

- The body of Christ desperately needs more role models. Are you one of them?
- Examine your heart in prayer to see if the Lord is calling you to coach, mentor, and disciple guys/girls.
- Being a role model is an honor and a privilege, but it also comes with a lot of responsibility and accountability.
- If you are a mature and seasoned married couple, start looking for at least one other couple to mentor and disciple.
- If you are an engaged or newlywed couple, be on the lookout for a seasoned couple to mentor you.
- If your local church does not have a ministry for couples or pre-marriage classes, ask your pastor to seriously get the ball rolling in this vital sphere.

21
KINGDOM CULTURE

What exactly is kingdom culture? God's way of life! Kingdom culture also refers to God's laws and standards for living on Earth. Kingdom culture is how God's children must think and behave, and kingdom culture is the language we must speak, which is vastly different from the rest of the world.

Kingdom culture, like any other national culture, has its own distinct qualities and characteristics. However, one issue here is that many of God's children are unaware of their kingdom culture, or they are living outside the boundaries of the kingdom culture. When this happens, they begin to lose the privileges, blessings, and protection that come as a standard for all kingdom citizens. And in this chapter, I want to emphasize how important it is for you to understand that you are a child of God, not of this world, and that we do not live by the standards or principles of this corrupt world, but rather by a different system and structure with which we align our thinking and lifestyle.

KINGDOM THINKING

In the kingdom culture, we have a completely different mindset and thinking. For we have the mind of Christ,[1] and need to align our thinking with His thinking. Additionally, the author of Hebrews challenges us with these words: "Don't copy the behavior and customs of this world, but let God transform you into a new person by changing the way you think. Then you will learn to know God's will for you, which is good and pleasant and perfect."[2]

The few powerful suggestions were to not imitate worldly behavior and to allow God, your Creator, to transform us, which happens through a new way of thinking. This new way of thinking is known as kingdom thinking. As we tune our hearts and minds to the living Word of God and the voice of the Holy Spirit, we will begin to do what the Bible teaches us and to obey that gentle inner voice that will begin to shape our mind into Christ's mind.

And this same kingdom thinking was in Daniel, who chose not to submit to the king's new decree forbidding anyone from praying, and this was the same kingdom thinking in the three Hebrew friends who chose not to bow down to the golden idol, and this was even more evident in the life of Jesus, who ignored religious voices that commanded Him to stop healing and doing supernatural works of God on the sabbath day. And this should be true for all of us as we reject what worldly ideology tries to teach us about dating, relationships, marriage, and sexual purity.

<blockquote>"KINGDOM THINKING IS TO HAVE THE MIND OF CHRIST, AND THIS WILL REQUIRE A CONTINUOUS RENEWAL OF YOUR MIND UNTIL THE DAY YOU DIE."</blockquote>

KINGDOM BEHAVIOR AND LIFESTYLE

We have a distinct kingdom culture that is markedly different from the culture of this world. In our kingdom culture, we do not engage in inappropriate behavior with people of the opposite sex. We have no sexual relations prior to marriage. When we get married, we do so as virgins. And, once again, the Apostle Paul challenges us with the following words: "Get rid of all bitterness, rage, anger, harsh words, and slander, as well as all types of evil behavior."[3]

The main takeaway is to eliminate "all types of evil behavior." Sexual promiscuity, adultery, fornication, and other forms of sexual immorality are examples of this behavior. And Sodom and Gomorrah are great examples of those who lived and behaved in such sexual perversion that God wanted to make an example of these two well-known cities in those days by burning them to cinders.

As God's children, our behavior and lifestyle must stand out like a bold statement, so that others will recognize, not second guess, but genuinely see that we are different. Some will mock and laugh at our righteous behavior, while others will inquire. In any case, we are commanded by God's living Word not to conform to this world, but to allow the light of His kingdom to shine in and through us all.

"KINGDOM BEHAVIOR AND LIFESTYLE ARE NOT OPTIONAL FOR THOSE WHO WANT TO BE A PART OF GOD'S KINGDOM."

KINGDOM LAWS AND STANDARDS

Every country has its own set of laws and regulations that apply to its citizens. A specific law in one country allows their citizens to do certain things, whereas the same action is forbidden in the next country, and those who are allowed to do what their country permits will be arrested in another. This principle is also unique to America, which is made up of fifty states, and while most laws are similar in each state, there are some that differ.

This is especially true when it comes to kingdom laws and standards. Worldly laws allow and even encourage having sex with whomever you want, whereas God's law strictly prohibits any form of sexual behavior for those who are not lawfully and legally married. The world's standards allow you to lust, covet another man's wife, fulfill your sexual appetites, commit adultery and fornication, whereas kingdom laws teach you to be holy, to keep your sexual purity until marriage, to be content with your spouse, and to only fulfill your sexual desires within the confines of a marriage convent.

And, while worldly law allows and even encourages you to divorce your spouse if you feel you are no longer compatible or have found another person who best suits your selfish desires, the law of His Word teaches us to remain faithful to our spouses and to learn how to serve one another, just as Christ serves His bride, the church. And this is only a brief summary of the stark differences between the twisted laws of this perverse world and the laws and standards of the kingdom.

"GOD ESTABLISHED KINGDOM LAWS AND STANDARDS TO PROTECT AND PRESERVE YOU, NOT TO BIND AND CONTROL YOU."

KINGDOM LANGUAGE

Each culture or nation has its own language or dialect. This also applies to those who are a part of God's kingdom, which has its own language. So, what distinguishes the kingdom language from the worldly language? Our words must be filled with life, purpose, purity, and honor, all of which come from within our inner spirit man, whereas the world speaks in the language of their flesh, which is full of pervasiveness, dishonor, and sexual comments, and is fed by the spirit of this world.

The words we speak will either bring us life or bring us destruction and curses. And if we are born-again and consider ourselves to be God's children, we will never say or do anything sexually perverse to the opposite gender. Or engage in sexually immoral conversations with our friends. And we can easily forget the dire warning that James issued: "And the tongue is a fire, a world of iniquity. The tongue is so set among our members that it defiles the whole body, and sets on fire the course of nature; and it is set on fire by hell. For every kind of beast and bird, of reptile and creature of the seas, is tamed and has been tamed by mankind. Bit no man can tame the tongue. It is an unruly evil, full of deadly poison. With it we bless our God and Father, and with it we curse men, who have been made in the similitude of God. Out of the same mouth proceed blessing and cursing. My brethren, these things ought not be so."[4]

"KINGDOM LANGUAGE IS A LANGUAGE OF LIFE, TRUTH, AND EDIFICATION, AS WELL AS GOD'S HEARTBEAT."

KINGDOM CITIZENS

To be a kingdom citizen, you must have a kingdom passport and abide by kingdom laws. And this passport is the Holy Spirit who lives within us, and the kingdom laws are God's living Word. And those who consider themselves to be kingdom citizens allow the Holy Spirit to govern them while also living in accordance with the truth as outlined in the Bible.

And the governor, the Holy Spirit, and the King, Jesus, rule in their kingdom according to different principles, and anyone who wishes to be a part of this kingdom must submit to these kingdom principles. Furthermore, the kingdom law book states:

"Above all, you must live as citizens of heaven, conducting yourselves in a manner worthy of the Good News about Christ."[5] The direct command is for us to live as citizens of heaven.

Sodom and Gomorrah are excellent examples of citizens who lived in opposition to what citizens of God's kingdom must do. This world's citizens have sex before marriage, but the kingdom's citizens do not. The citizens of this world have lustful appetites for the opposite gender, but kingdom citizens honor one another and do not covet what is not theirs. And the citizens of this world indulge in the desires of their carnal minds, whereas the citizens of heaven indulge in the desires of the King and His kingdom.

As I warp up the pages of this *Rated R* book, my dear precious brother and sister in Christ, I want to both challenge and bless you. I challenge you to make today the start of your new journey as a single person who will choose to live a life of sexual purity in accordance with God's living Word. But if you are married, keep your marriage covenant and be a living example of what a kingdom marriage looks like to others. And I want to bless you, my friend, so that you will become a Godly man or woman on this earth who lives by kingdom principles and desires God's kingdom to abide within you and shine through you, so that others will see it and desire what you have.

"KINGDOM CITIZENS ARE PART OF THE HEAVENLY CULTURE, AND THEY HAVE THE PRIVILEGE AND HONOR OF REPRESENTING THE KING ON THIS EARTH."

RATED "R" RECOMMENDATIONS

- Kingdom culture is not a theological theory, but a revelation that every born-again individual needs to grasp.
- Kingdom thinking is to have the mind of Christ, which is rooted in the Word of God.
- Kingdom behavior and lifestyle are what will set you apart from the rest of the crowd.
- Kingdom laws and standards are derived from the living Word of God, so start digging deep.
- Kingdom language is a language that is full of life, hope, motivation, edification, and love.
- Kingdom citizens are well aware that they must submit to King Jesus, obey the governor, who is the Holy Spirit, and faithfully adhere to the kingdom laws outlined in the Bible.

NOTES

Chapter 1

1. 1 Corinthians 1:23
2. Genesis 2:18

Chapter 2

1. Genesis 2:25
2. Songs of S 8:4 (NIV)

Chapter 3

1. https://www.thesaurus.com/browse/evolution
2. https://www.britannica.com/topic/pornography
3. www.Pornhub.com
4. www.Pornhub.com
5. www.Pornhub.com
6. www.Pornhub.com
7. www.Pornhub.com
8. www.Pornhub.com
9. Genesis 1:27
10. Genesis 3:1
11. Psalm 139:14 (MSG)
12. 1 Corinthians 6:19-20

Chapter 5

1. Hebrews 10:26-27
2. https://www.thesaurus.com/browse/willful
3. 2 Corinthians 5:17
4. Romans 6:12-14

Chapter 6

1. 1 Corinthians 6:16 (NIV)
2. https://www.cdc.gov/tobacco/data_statistics/fact_shee ts/secondhand_smoke/heal th_effects/index.htm
3. Romans 12:2
4. Mark 10:7-8
5. 1 Corinthians 6:18

Chapter 7

1. https://www.yourdictionary.com/gram
2. https://www.businessofapps.com/data/tik-tok-statistics/

Chapter 8

1. 1 Timothy 4:12 (NLT)
2. Proverbs 5:15-18 (NLT)
3. Deuteronomy 22:13-19

Chapter 9

1. 1 Corinthians 7:1

Chapter 10

1. 2 Corinthians 6:14–15 (NLT)
2. 1 Samuel 13:14
3. Gal 6:7-9)

Chapter 11

1. Ecclesiastes 3:1
2. Songs of Solomon 8:4 (MSG)
3. Genesis 2:15 (NIV)
4. Genesis 2:18 (NLT)
5. Proverbs 16:9
6. Proverbs 19:21
7. Matthew 6:33

Chapter 12

1. Genesis 2:18 (NLT)
2. Matthew 5:31-32

Chapter 13

1. Genesis 2:18 (NLT)
2. Genesis 2:18a (NLT emphasis added)
3. 1 Peter 3:7 (NLT)
4. 1 Timothy 5:8
5. Genesis 2:18
6. 1 Corinthians 7:39
7. https://en.wiktionary.org/wiki/compatible
8. Ecclesiastes 4:9-12

Chapter 14

1. https://www.goldbergjones-sandiego.com/divorce/video-games-impact-divorce/
2. https://www.livescience.com/65580-video-game-addiction-mental-health-disorder.html#:~:text=Recently%2C%20the%20WHO%20officially%20recognized,to%20count%20as%20a%20disorder.

Chapter 15

1. https://www.youtube.com/watch?v=zFUM_Dya7U8
2. 1 Corinthians 15:33 (NIV)

Chapter 16

1. https://www.cdc.gov/nchs/fastats/marriage-divorce.htm
2. 1 Corinthians 7:32-33 (NLT)
3. 1 Corinthians 7:34b

Chapter 17

1. Matthew 7:15

Chapter 18

1. 1 Corinthians 7:1

Chapter 20

1. https://www.dictionary.com/browse/role-model
2. Proverbs 27:17
3. 2 Timothy 2:15
4. https://www.dictionary.com/browse/approved
https://www.thesaurus.com/browse/approved

Chapter 21

1. 1 Corinthians 2:16
2. Hebrews 12:2 (NLT)
3. Ephesians 4:31 (NLT)
4. James 3:6-10
5. Philippians 1:27a (NLT)

ABOUT THE AUTHOR

Stan is an entrepreneur, author, life coach, and vlogger. He is passionate in helping others to discover and understand their identity in Christ through coaching, mentoring, and discipleship.

StanBelyshev.com

OTHER BOOKS BY THE AUTHOR

Generation Gap
Raising The Next Generation of Leaders

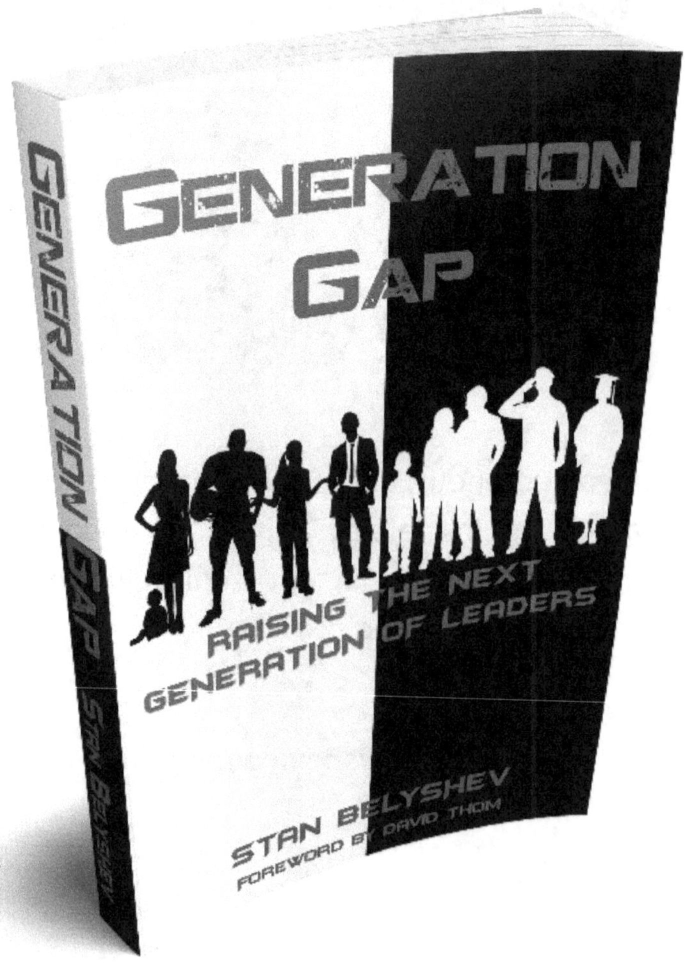

Can I See Your ID?
Discovering And Understanding Your Purpose and Identity

Know your Identity in Christ!
Know your Identity through Christ!

God Is...Good
No Matter What God Is A Good God

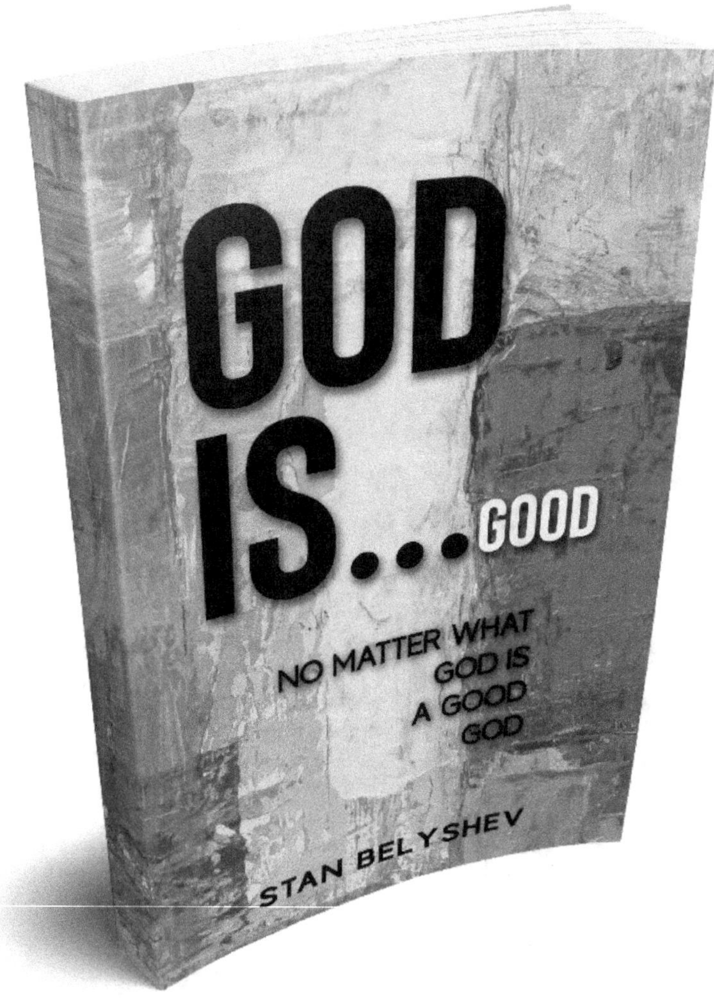

Is God A Good God?

When Life Is Full of It

An Antidote For Your Mind

"Our world is already full of it, so please do not be a contributor."

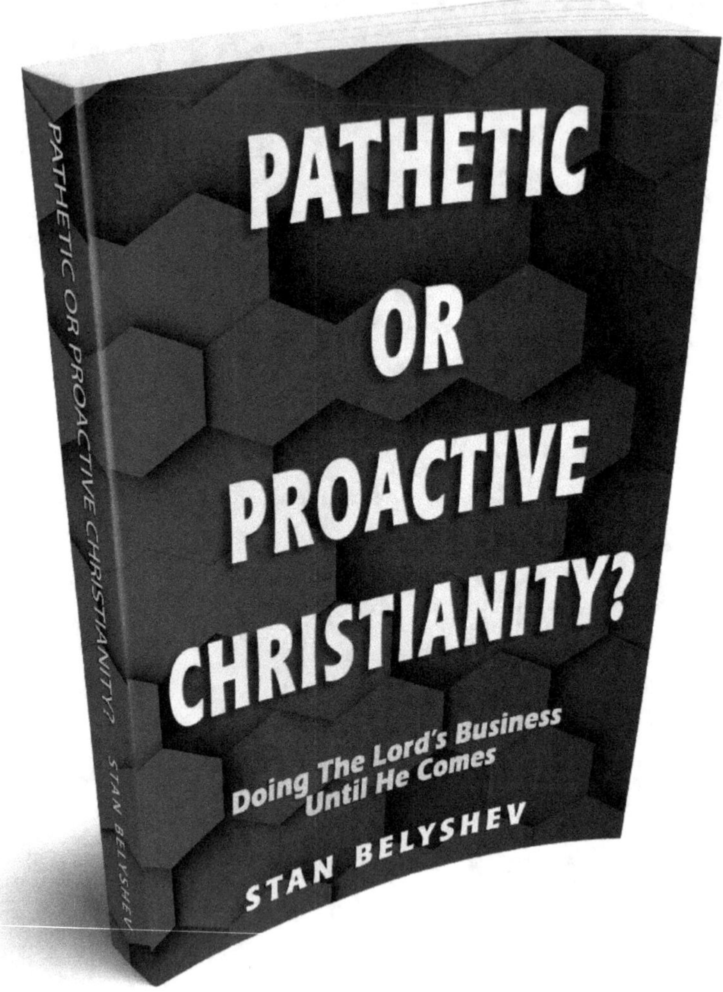

Are you a pathetic or a proactive Christian?

RATED R - *Spanish Version*

Una Perspectiva Bíblica Sobre las Citas, las Relaciones, el Matrimonio, y la Pureza Sexual

(Spanish Edition)